BISMARCK

BISMARCK

THE CHASE AND SINKING OF HITLER'S GOLIATH

BRITANNIA NAVAL HISTORIES OF WORLD WAR II

University of Plymouth Press

This edition first published in the United Kingdom in 2012 by University of Plymouth Press, Portland Square, Drake Circus, Plymouth, Devon, PL4 8AA, United Kingdom.

Paperback   ISBN 978-1-84102-326-7
Hardback   ISBN 978-1-84102-327-4

A CIP catalogue record of this book is available from the British Library.

Publisher: Paul Honeywill
Commissioning Editor: Charlotte Carey
Editor: Miranda Spicer
Series Editors: G. H. Bennett, J. E. Harrold, R. Porter and M. J. Pearce
Publishing Assistant: Maxine Aylett

Historical content courtesy of Britannia Museum, Britannia Royal Naval College, Dartmouth, TQ6 0HJ.

Cover image © Edward Stables 2012

Typeset by University of Plymouth Press in Janson 10/14pt.
Printed by Short Run Press, Exeter, United Kingdom.

The historical documents reproduced here appear as unedited text, apart from minor changes made to date formats and corrections to typing errors found in the original.

Britannia Royal Naval College

A majestic landmark, which towers above the harbour town of Dartmouth in Devon, Britannia Royal Naval College was designed by royal architect Sir Aston Webb to project an image of British sea power. A fine example of Edwardian architecture, the College has prepared future generations of officers for the challenges of service and leadership since 1905.

The Britannia Museum opened in 1999 to safeguard the College's rich collection of historic artefacts, art and archives and promote greater public understanding of Britain's naval and maritime heritage, as a key element in the development of British history and culture. It also aims to instil a sense of identity and ethos in the Officer Cadets that pass through the same walls as their forbears, from great admirals to national heroes, to royalty.

www.royalnavy.mod.uk/The-Fleet/Shore-Establishments/BRNC-Dartmouth

Contents

Foreword

Commander Nigel Ward

The immensely powerful German battleship, *Bismarck*, posed a significant threat to Britain's endeavours to win the Battle of the Atlantic. When, in a short exchange of fire, she sank the pride of the Royal Navy, HMS *Hood*, alarm bells rang throughout Whitehall and in the War Cabinet.

Britain's lifeblood depended upon its control of the seas and this was already being severely threatened by the U-boat offensive against British shipping convoys. *Bismarck* added to this threat in a most significant way and if she had been allowed to roam the Atlantic unhindered, there would have been little hope left for the survival of British merchant fleets. The sinking of *Bismarck* became a top priority in the war effort. There was no way around it: she had to be hunted down and destroyed as soon as possible.

Tracking her position and intended movement was a remarkable achievement in itself. There were no satellites available and the extensive pre-war investment in land-based aircraft was found to be distinctly lacking in the context of maritime surveillance and air warfare. It was as though a 'sea blindness' had infected Whitehall. The concentration of resources on land-based air power demonstrated that the British Government had lost sight of its heritage as an Island Nation – dependent upon the sea for all imports and commercial needs.

This negligence on the part of the British Government and military leaders was deplorable. As Winston Churchill had noted:

> "Whereas any European power has to support a vast army first of all, we in this fortunate, happy island, relieved by our insular position of a double burden, may turn our undivided efforts and attention to the Fleet. Why should we sacrifice a game in which we are sure to win to play a game in which we are bound to lose?"

His words were ignored and so later he reinforced his statement with the following:

> "Nothing, nothing in the world, nothing that you may think of or dream of, or anyone else may tell you: no argument, however seductive, must lead you to abandon that Naval supremacy on which the life of our country depends."

In spite of such wisdom, Britain had failed to provide its aircraft carriers and the Royal Navy Fleet Air Arm with modern combat aircraft (the United States and the Japanese had made no such mistake). Britain's ability to bring to action and destroy *Bismarck* was therefore in considerable doubt. The only air power that the Royal Navy could bring to bear against her was the ancient 'stringbag'; the Swordfish biplane that was limited to the slow speed delivery of a single torpedo. Naval intelligence and expertise had already achieved the near impossible – they had found her. Could they now engage and destroy her?

Against all odds, the Swordfish aircrew in their open cockpits pressed home their torpedo attacks through a veritable storm of accurate anti-aircraft fire from *Bismarck*. The thick armour surrounding her hull below the waterline was enough to protect her and her crew from torpedo impact. But then one lone torpedo struck her Achilles heel, her rudder and associated steering gear. The bravery and daring of the Swordfish pilots had paid off and *Bismarck* had been virtually immobilised. She became a sitting target for the surface fleet and was duly dispatched.

Following this remarkable achievement, very soon, Britain's aircraft carriers were provided with modern, 'state-of-the-art' fighters and fighter-bombers from the United States. Many years later, 'sea blindness' returned to Whitehall during the Cold War period when Britain's aircraft carriers were withdrawn from service.

By contrast, a 'foot in the door' was provided by the Sea Harriers embarked in HMS *Invincible*. Fleet Air Arm pilots had just 20 aircraft when they sailed South in 1982 with the naval task force to retake the Falkland Islands following the invasion by Argentina. They were outnumbered by 200 Argentine combat aircraft and there was no possibility of effective support from the land-based Royal Air Force – because there were no bases for the latter to fly from.

The air war over the Falklands was conducted predominantly by the Royal Navy Fleet Air Arm and victory was only made possible by the Sea Harrier. Contrary to what was announced by Royal Air Force public relations, the RAF contributed little more to that victory than to the demise of *Bismarck*. Navy Sea Harriers shot down 25 enemy aircraft and established air supremacy over the Islands – allowing courageous British ground forces to complete their victory. Published and reprinted twice, *Sea Harrier over the Falklands*[1] tells the story in full detail and it is an account of the air war, which has not been challenged by the Ministry of Defence or any other informed source.

It is almost beyond belief that in spite of the many historical successes that have been achieved by the Royal Navy and her carrier air groups since World War II, the British Government has accepted the decision of the Strategic Defence and Security Review 2010 to gap Britain's aircraft carrier capability until at least 2020.

The extraordinarily high cost of the UK land-based air campaign over Libya demonstrates the controversial choice of this way ahead, which has led to a major reduction in British military and political influence overseas.

Commander Nigel 'Sharkey' Ward DSC

1. Commander Ward, *Sea Harrier Over The Falklands: A Maverick at War*, Cassell Military Paperbacks, 2000.

Introduction

Dr G. H. Bennett,
Dr R. Bennett and
E. Bennett

"In brilliant sunshine – the 'Hitler weather' which traditionally favours any important event at which the Führer is present – the first of Germany's 35,000-ton battleships was to-day named *Bismarck* after the creator of the Second Reich, and watched by the makers of the Third Reich, moved down the Blohm and Voss slips to the sea. Hamburg had prepared a great welcome for Herr Hitler... The Führer reached the green launching platform immediately below the high bows of the new battleship... In a short speech Herr Hitler said that the fate of the German fleet, which was sunk 20 years ago after fighting gloriously for four years, still cut deep into the heart of every German. Nationalist-Socialist Germany, therefore, looked upon the resurrection of that Fleet with particular love and sympathy... 'As Führer of the German people and Chancellor of the Reich... I can give this ship no finer name from our history than the name of that man who, as a true knight without fear and reproach, was the creator of that German Empire whose resurrection from the direst misery and whose wonderful enlargement has been granted to us by Providence.'"[1]

From the moment of her launch, *Bismarck* was to become one of the most iconic battleships of the 20th century. Named after Otto von Bismarck, first Chancellor of the newly united Germany in 1871, the ship was the embodiment of German national pride. A leviathan displacing 50,900-tons and armed with eight 38-cm guns in four turrets, as well as formidable secondary armament, the ship marked almost the final stage in the evolution of the battleship. On her one-and-only war cruise, the pride of the German Navy destroyed HMS *Hood*, the pride of the Royal Navy, before *Bismarck* was reduced to a sinking hulk, on 27 May 1941, by British battleships and cruisers.

There were just 116 survivors from *Bismarck*'s crew of 2,200. Her destruction resulted in a strategic shift in the battle for the Atlantic. Hitler would never again countenance operations which would place the major units of the German surface fleet in the dangerous waters of the Atlantic Ocean. The German surface fleet would be relocated to the fjords of Norway and to the Baltic; these waters were considered far safer than those dominated by the Allied navies. Hitler's loss of confidence in the German surface fleet led, in due course, to a confrontation with Admiral Raeder, the head of the German Navy, and the near scrapping of the remaining battleships and cruisers of the Kriegsmarine.

The statistical and organisational details of *Bismarck*'s life emphasise her monumental scale. Laid down on 1 July 1936, *Bismarck* would be launched on 14 February 1939. It would take until 24 August 1940 for her to be commissioned. *Bismarck*'s main armoured belt was 32 cm thick. At 251 metres long and 36 metres across at the beam, *Bismarck*'s primary role was as a gun platform for her main armament. Designed in 1934, her main armament of eight 38-cm guns, operating in four twin turrets (Anton, Bruno, Caesar and Dora), were the heaviest guns to be installed on a German battleship. Each turret, operating on a roller-track platform, weighed 1056 metric tons. *Bismarck*'s crew was divided into 12 divisions (180–220 men):

Divisions 1–4: Main and secondary armament
Divisions 5–6: Anti-aircraft batteries
Division 7: Ancillary personnel (carpenters, stewards, cooks etc.)
Division 8: Artillery mechanical personnel
Division 9: Signallers and telegraphists
Divisions 10–12: Engineers, technicians and stokers

To spot the fall of shot for the main armament and to carry out localised reconnaissance, *Bismarck* carried four Arado AR196 floatplanes. They were stored in three hangars (two in the double 120-metre hanger by the main mast and two others in single 60-metre hangers amidships). The aircraft were catapult launched along a 32-metre double catapult. It had a telescopic function, which meant that it could be extended to 48 metres in length to cope with heavy payloads. Following launch, the aircraft would land on the sea to be brought aboard by crane. *Bismarck*'s power plant consisted of 12 boilers and three turbines. At an economical cruising speed of 16 knots (as opposed to a maximum of 30 knots) the ship could travel 9,280 nautical miles on a full fuel load of 8,294 metric tons. Three FuMO 23 radars would help to guide the battleship on its journey. At every turn, the facts and figures of Battleship *Bismarck* emphasised her formidable size and fearsome spectacle. Her total cost was 197 million Reichsmarks.

British reactions to the launch of *Bismarck* varied considerably. Within Royal Navy and shipbuilding circles there was considerable scepticism about German claims that the ship displaced only 35,000 tons. Among the circles of appeasers in pre-war Britain some hope was invested in the name given to the battleship. *The Times* newspaper commented:

"There is perhaps some significance in the name given to the first of

Germany's new great battleships. She and her consort, which is to be launched shortly, are built under the provisions of the Anglo-German naval agreement of 35 per cent of British tonnage. That limit, as far as battleships are concerned, would hardly be reached if Germany's present battle fleet, built and building, were to be doubled. It may be thought symbolic therefore that the new ship should be named after the Chancellor who always set his face against naval rivalry with Great Britain."[2]

The impressive nature and importance of Battleship *Bismarck* has resulted in a small cottage industry, publishing books on the story of the ship.[3] Her story is well known, but in the re-telling, some aspects of her life and destruction have been obscured. Several aspects of *Bismarck*'s story deserve greater clarity, including the Kriegsmarine's purpose in building *Bismarck*; the purpose of *Bismarck*'s mission; and the decisions taken during her war cruise. Unfortunately, many aspects of her final mission cannot be resolved. The senior officers onboard, who took the critical decisions in 1941, did not survive her final battle, and because of the need to maintain radio silence, the radio transmissions from *Bismarck* are not illuminating. However, alongside the battle summary which follows, relevant sections from meetings held by Hitler, known as the Führer Conferences, appear. This gives the German context and reveals comments minuted at the time.

The Kriegsmarine's Purpose in Building *Bismarck*

Battleship *Bismarck* was part of Germany's Plan Z developed in the 1930s. Plan Z was a blueprint designed to give the German Navy a fleet able to compete against the British for control of the seas by 1944. *Bismarck*, and her sister ship *Tirpitz*, were to be Germany's first true battleships of the new era. The *Bismarck* class would in turn be surpassed by battleships of even bigger design.[4] However, the outbreak of war in 1939 interrupted the development of the balanced fleet. Along with the rest of Germany's surface fleet, *Bismarck* and *Tirpitz* would be used in the campaign against British commerce, the convoys and merchant ships on which the British war economy depended, instead of fighting as elements of a balanced surface fleet operating under air cover provided by the aircraft carrier *Graf Zepplin*. *Bismarck* was to be put to a purpose for which she had never been intended. As the battleship worked up in the Baltic in 1940 and early 1941, three questions dominated the thinking in the Admiralty in London:

1. When would *Bismarck* be sent into the Atlantic to attack the North American convoys?
2. Which route might she take?
3. Would she sail on her own or as part of a task force?

Purpose of *Bismarck*'s Mission

As Admiral Kranke later noted, during 1941 it was envisaged that *Bismarck* would operate as part of a task force in the Atlantic.

> "The idea was to form a powerful group in the Atlantic, made up of the *Bismarck* and *Prinz Eugen*, with the *Scharnhorst* and *Gneisenau*, which would be in a position to attack convoys escorted by battleships. Unfortunately, an aircraft carrier was lacking. The group was not to be scattered."[5]

However, damage to *Scharnhorst* and *Gneisenau* following a sortie into the Atlantic in 1940 were to rule them out of operations for much of 1941. In May 1941, *Bismarck* and *Prinz Eugen* would sail alone. But why were they allowed to depart – a pair of ships instead of part of a powerful battle squadron? Undoubtedly pressure of events played a key part in the timing of the operation. *Bismarck*'s war cruise had begun on 18 May, two days before the launch of Operation Mercury: the invasion of Crete. This was to start with the landing of paratroops with further troops landing by sea. It was realised at the outset that such was the Royal Navy's strength in the Mediterranean that the sea-borne element of the operation might be seriously contested. It was therefore imperative to draw some of that strength out of the Mediterranean. An operation in the Atlantic involving *Bismarck* could provide the necessary diversion to draw off the Royal Navy's Force H from Gibraltar.[6]

The instructions given to Admiral Luetjens, commanding the task force, were explicit. As Admiral Assmann later explained:

> "Enemy supply traffic in the Atlantic north of the equator was to be attacked. The operation (codename Rheinuebung) was to last as long as the situation permitted. The route out to the Atlantic was through

the Great Belt, the Skagerrak, and the Norwegian Sea. The ships were to attempt a breakthrough unobserved, the mission remained as defined in the operational directive. It was left to the discretion of the Fleet Commander to shorten or break off the operation as the situation developed. According to the Group's directive the main aim throughout the entire operation was the destruction of enemy shipping. As far as possible, they were to shun risks which would jeopardise the operation. Hence they were to avoid encounters with ships of equal strength. If an encounter were inevitable then it should be an all-out engagement."[7]

Loss of the *Hood*

On 18 May 1941, *Bismarck*, together with the heavy cruiser *Prinz Eugen*, sailed from Gotenhafen, putting into Kors fjord near Bergen on 21 May. The British quickly became aware that *Bismarck* was at sea and the Royal Navy made its dispositions accordingly. *Bismarck*'s location was confirmed at 2015 on 23 May when the two German ships were spotted by the cruiser HMS *Norfolk* in the Denmark Strait. As Admiral Assmann later related, the encounter with *Norfolk* was entirely unexpected:

"Considering the general evaluation of the enemy disposition, the encounter with an enemy cruiser patrol in the Denmark Straits to a certain extent came as a surprise to the Fleet Commander, but owing to the complete calm in the enemy radio traffic there was no reason to suppose that any extensive enemy operation was under way to prevent a suspected German advance into the Atlantic. When cruisers *Scheer* and *Hipper* made a breakthrough via the Denmark Straits on their return from the Atlantic, they had also noticed heavy cruisers on patrol and were able to elude the enemy in good time... What was most surprising, and of decisive importance for the further course of the operation, was the probability, established for the first time, that the enemy possessed evidently excellently functioning radar equipment."[8]

Following the encounter between *Norfolk* and *Bismarck*, HMS *Hood*, together with Britain's newest battleship HMS *Prince of Wales*, moved to intercept the German units. *Hood* was of World War I vintage and *Prince of Wales* was still not fully operational. The two forces met on 24 May in an engagement which was to be as short as it was dramatic. As the British ships attempted to close the range on *Bismarck* and *Prinz Eugen*, the British and German vessels began firing at each other. Suddenly *Hood* was struck by one or more shells. Onboard the heavy cruiser HMS *Suffolk*, a young Polish officer witnessed what happened next on *Hood*. "We saw the flash of a bursting shell hit the dark silhouette of the *Hood* and the next moment a huge pillar of flame shot up to the sky. A black cloud covered part of the horizon like a blanket. We could sense something terrible had happened. The guns of the *Hood* were silent."[9]

Onboard *Prince of Wales*, anxious observers, including a Reuters correspondent, peered in the direction of *Hood*:

"There was a terrific explosion, and the whole of the vast ship was enveloped in a flash of flame and smoke which rose high into the air in the shape of a giant mushroom. Sections of funnels, masts and other parts were hurled hundreds of feet into the sky, some falling on the ship. *Hood*'s bow tilted vertically into the air, and three or four minutes after she was hit all that remained, apart from bits of wreckage, was a flicker of flame and smoke on the water's surface."[10]

Hood was gone and only three survivors of a crew of 1,421 remained to be pulled out of the water.[11] Outgunned, outnumbered, and suffering from a series of mechanical problems, *Prince of Wales* turned away, leaving the British heavy cruisers to keep a long-range watch on the two German vessels.[12] The destruction of *Hood* was a remarkable triumph for the Kriegsmarine, but it was not entirely without cost: *Bismarck* had been damaged and was leaking fuel.

Alternative courses of action were considered onboard the ship and in Berlin. Having scored such a major victory, should *Bismarck* and *Prinz Eugen* return to Norwegian waters, or should they press on further into the Atlantic and try to reach one of the German-controlled ports along the French coast? Admirals Schniewind and Schuster later revealed to British interrogators:

"In the course of the *Bismarck* operation, after the battle with the *Hood*, discussions arose in the naval staff as to whether it was not better to order the battleship to return to the Norwegian coast. This breakthrough appeared more feasible than continuing the operation or making for Brest... The naval supreme commander [Grand Admiral Raeder] refused to commit himself to issuing definite instructions to the battleship or the group command directing the operation, because he was not sufficiently well informed as to the battleship's condition and radius of action and did not wish to hamper the free decisions of the commander in chief of all of the fleet and the group command."[13]

The Chase

As *Bismarck* and her consort pushed further into the Atlantic,[14] the battleship became the target for an aerial attack by torpedo-carrying Swordfish bi-planes flying from HMS *Victorious*. *Bismarck* was hit by at least one torpedo although the damage was minimal. Shortly afterwards, *Bismarck* turned to engage the British heavy cruisers shadowing her. The move was a distraction which allowed the *Prinz Eugen* to break away and move away unobserved. *Bismarck* too, on a different course, was able to slip away from her shadowing escorts. It was over 31 hours later that *Bismarck* was spotted by a shore-based Catalina flying boat. This allowed the Royal Navy to concentrate resources against the German vessel. Increasingly, senior officers in the Admiralty were convinced that *Bismarck* was heading for the safety of Brest; the only question was whether they could bring her to action before she reached port. Two attacks were launched by the Fleet Air Arm on 26 May: the first almost sank the cruiser HMS *Sheffield* in a case of mistaken identity.[15] The second attack, at 2047, crippled *Bismarck*, which was hit by two or three torpedoes. A lucky hit jammed *Bismarck*'s steering gear, condemning her to steam round in circles. Desperate attempts to free the steering gear were only partially successful. Although attempts were made to send U-boats to *Bismarck*'s aid in Berlin, on the ship, it was recognised that nothing could be done to prevent the British from closing in.

The Destruction of *Bismarck*

Catching up with the crippled battleship through the night of 26/27 May, the British battleships opened fire on the still-circling *Bismarck* at 0847 on 27 May. The battle ended as a contest approximately 40 minutes after it had begun. The opening of *Bismarck*'s final battle was relayed to *The War Illustrated* by an un-named officer on HMS *King George V*:

> "I have my glasses on *Bismarck*. She fires all four guns from her two forward turrets, four thin orange flames. The Germans have a reputation for hitting with their early salvoes. Now I know what suspended animation

means. It seems to take about two hours for those shots to fall! The splashes shoot up opposite but beyond *Rodney*'s fo'c'sle. I'm sorry to say that we all thought, 'Thank heavens she's shooting at *Rodney*'. My second thought was that I wouldn't care to be facing nine 16-inch and ten 14-inch guns; I just kept my binoculars glued to *Bismarck*. *Rodney*'s first salvo produced great white columns of water 120 ft. high that would break the back of a destroyer and sink her like a stone if she steamed through one of them. The second splash I missed – all except one shot which seemed to belong to *King George V* and was a little ahead of *Bismarck*. Then I watched *Rodney* to see if she was being hit, but she just sat there like a great slab of rock blocking the northern horizon, and suddenly belched a full salvo. I actually saw their projectiles flying through the air for some seconds after they left the guns like little diminishing footballs curving up and up into the sky. Now, I am sure that four or five hit. There was only one great splash, and a sort of flurry of spray and splash which might have been a waterline hit. The others had bored their way through the *Krupp* armour belt like cheese; and pray God I may never know what they did as they exploded inside the hull."[16]

Forty minutes later, firing from *Bismarck* had all but ceased. The British battleships continued to pound the blazing *Bismarck*, which stubbornly refused to sink. A Polish officer onboard HMS *Rodney* observed:

"I can count the holes made by our shells on her starboard side. More than fifteen. Some are still smoking, while others just gape emptily... The enemy is no longer firing. She has been silenced by the fire of the British guns. I have never seen such a great ship; ideally proportioned, a long bow, a well-balanced bridge even though now in ruins."[17]

Shortage of fuel forced *Rodney* and the other British battleships to break off their attack at 1015, while the cruiser HMS *Dorsetshire* and the *Tribal* class destroyer HMS *Maori* were sent in to finish with torpedoes. *Dorsetshire* rescued just 111 men before the warning of a U-boat in the vicinity forced her to cease rescue work (one survivor died onboard *Dorsetshire* as a result of his wounds). Later that day, U-74 picked up a further three survivors from a carley float that they had managed to launch. On 28 May, the German weather ship *Sachsenwald* picked up the final two survivors.

As *Bismarck* finally slipped beneath the waves, news of her sinking was signalled to London to be announced in the House of Commons by a jubilant Winston Churchill. A decisive British victory had been achieved in difficult circumstances. Chance had played a major role in allowing the British to re-acquire the German vessel and to stop her just at the point when it seemed certain that she would escape to the safety of Brest. The chase and sinking of *Bismarck* was followed eagerly by the world's press.[18] In the United States the victory was taken as evidence that despite the threat of the U-boat, the Royal Navy had held the upper hand in the North Atlantic.

Hitler was deeply affected by the loss of *Bismarck*. He had been elated when Grand Admiral Raeder had telephoned to tell him of the victory over HMS *Hood*, but had grown steadily more concerned and depressed as *Bismarck* was chased towards her final battle. The final message from *Bismarck* had expressed undimmed confidence in Hitler's leadership and certainty about the final victory of Germany over her enemies. Hitler had replied in emotional tones: "All Germany is with you. What can be done is being done. The fulfilment of your duty will fortify our people in the struggle for their existence".[19] Following the loss of the battleship, Hitler had been silent until he asked for details of how many crew had been onboard. Reflecting on the scale of the losses, he declared that he would never again sanction the deployment of one of Germany's remaining surface ships to the Atlantic. Only the safe arrival of *Prinz Eugen* at Brest on 1 June relieved the gloom. Entering port she steamed past the mooring buoys, which had been put out to receive *Bismarck*.[20] At his meeting with Grand Admiral Raeder on 6 June, the Führer made no secret of his displeasure at the loss of *Bismarck*.[21]

Winston Churchill was in no doubt either about the importance of *Bismarck*'s sinking. On 28 May, he sent a telegraph to President Roosevelt of the United States highlighting the fact that the Royal Navy was now free to deploy a number of battleships, previously forced to remain at the Scapa Flow anchorage to meet any sortie by the German battleship. Churchill considered that this in turn could materially affect the situation in the Far East, where Britain and the US faced a threat of war with the Japanese who were eager to expand their Empire.[22] With the Royal Navy perhaps freer to move some of its capital ships to Asian waters, the Japanese might prove more reluctant to run the risk of war with the British and American navies.[23] Churchill later wrote that sinking *Bismarck* was of global significance for the British Empire, while at the same time hinting at the inter-service rivalry which had broken out over the relative levels of credit which the Royal Navy and Royal Air Force could claim for finding and sinking the German battleship:

> "Had she escaped, the moral effects of her continuing existence as much as the material damage she might have inflicted on our shipping would have been calamitous. Many misgivings would have arisen regarding our capacity to control the oceans, and these would have been trumpeted round the world to our great detriment and discomfort. All branches rightly claimed their share in the successful outcome."[24]

Post War Controversies

The inter-service rivalry came to a head during 1946, in the lead-up to the publication of the official dispatch dealing with *Bismarck*. There was considerable resentment within the Air Ministry at the limited references in the dispatch to the efforts of Coastal Command to locate the battleship.[25] Representatives of the Air Ministry politely reminded the Admiralty that, but for the aircraft of Coastal Command, the battleships of the Royal Navy would not have been able to re-acquire *Bismarck* during the extended hunt.[26] Senior figures within the RAF considered that the lack of reference to the efforts and success of Coastal Command were intended to garner for the senior service the maximum credit for the sinking of *Bismarck*. That, in turn, would serve as a distraction for the sinking of HMS *Hood* and its immediate aftermath. In truth, the *Bismarck* episode was a powerful reminder of the results that could be achieved by effective co-operation between the Royal Air Force and Royal Navy. It also underlined the vital importance of an effective Fleet Air Arm operating from carriers able to protect a fleet and to provide strike forces well beyond the range of land-based aircraft. The disagreement over the official dispatch was kept 'in-house' between the Royal Air Force and Royal Navy, but another controversy was to run for longer.

Shortly after the stories of her sinking began to circulate, it seemed that *Bismarck* may not have been sunk by the guns and torpedoes of the Royal Navy but had, in fact, been scuttled by her own crew. Following interrogation of *Bismarck*'s survivors, the Department of Naval Intelligence was ready to conclude that, while there was no certainty about what had caused the vessel to sink, some of the prisoners had stated that scuttling charges had certainly hastened the process. While some later accounts would portray the scuttling of *Bismarck* as a final act of defiance, on a par with the scuttling of the Kaiser's High Seas Fleet in 1919, the Department of Naval Intelligence viewed the matter rather differently. Evidence from survivors pointed towards a breakdown in morale onboard the doomed battleship that had affected all ranks from Admiral Günther Luetjens downwards.[27] Observers of the final action against *Bismarck* provided further evidence that seemed to confirm this breakdown:

"The action had been going perhaps twenty minutes; some of her secondary armament and certainly two of the great turrets were still firing, perhaps a little wildly, for nobody on our side showed signs of a hit. There, racing across her quarterdeck were little human figures; one climbed over the wire guard rails, hung on with one hand, looked back, and then jumped into the sea. Others just jumped without looking back at all – a little steady trickle of them jumping into the sea one after another."[28]

Under interrogation, survivors embittered by what they saw as the abandonment of *Bismarck* by the Luftwaffe and U-boat arm made statements that indicated that crews had abandoned their guns and that, in at least one case, an officer had shot down some of the crew in a vain effort to get them to stay at their posts. Other accounts refer to groups of men coming together in locations sheltered from the storm of shot to determine how they could escape the inferno. Herbert Manthey, who was one of the three men picked up by U-74, related how the anti-aircraft crews abandoned their guns in order to take shelter: "First I was with a group of 20 men in the aftergunnery position. After a few hits close by we fled behind the turrets C and D on the upper deck."[29] Stating that he and his two comrades were washed into the sea with a carley float, they were clearly some distance away from *Bismarck* when *Dorsetshire* closed in for the kill.

Despite the 'restricted' classification of the Department of Naval Intelligence's report on the *Bismarck* interrogation, rumours began to circulate in Britain about the collapse in morale on *Bismarck*, and the use of scuttling charges. In the House of Commons, Rear-Admiral Beamish made mention of the scuttling rumour in February 1942. He said:

"I would like to mention a rumour – it is nothing more than a rumour.

The other day somebody said to me, 'Didn't you know that they were never able to sink the *Bismarck*?' The *Bismarck*'s crew knew that they could not go on fighting, steaming, or escaping, and they were determined that the ship should not fall into the hands of the British because she was torpedo-proof, and therefore, they opened the seacocks and sank her."[30]

In 1989, the wreck of *Bismarck* was located and photographed by a team with Dr Robert Ballard at the head.[31] The wreck was mostly intact. Held in place by gravity, the four main turrets of the battleship had become detached from the hulk as soon as she rolled over and sank. Parts of the superstructure had broken away as the ship's underwater descent had accelerated. Hitting bottom with enormous force, the wreck had slid some distance before coming to rest. Most importantly, at some point in her journey beneath the sea, the last 35 ft of the stern had become detached. Some analysts have argued that this may indicate a flaw in the design of *Bismarck* and other German ships of the period – the stern of the *Prinz Eugen* suffered similar failure following a torpedo strike on 23 February 1942. Despite considerable damage inflicted during the final battle, the forward and the aft conning towers remain. The wreck was found to be in surprisingly good condition with much of the wooden deck panelling still in place. Sunk in mud almost to the waterline, Ballard's expedition did little to resolve the controversy over the precise cause of *Bismarck*'s sinking. However, Ballard did suggest that the lack of implosion damage, which results when a partially flooded hull reaches a depth where it can no longer survive the pressure, seemed to point in the direction of a gradual sinking and he concluded:

"We found no evidence on the wreck of the implosions that occur when a ship sinks before it is fully flooded. For an example of the two ways a ship can sink, you need only to look at the two main pieces of the *Titanic* hull as we found them on the ocean bottom. The bow, which had been opened up by the iceberg and filled with water over the two and a half hours between the impact and the final plunge, was virtually intact except for damage sustained when it hit the ocean floor. The stern, which had not been hit was only partly flooded when the ship broke in two and sank, was totally devastated, a chaos of twisted and torn hull plating. This was because the pressure of the water outside the hull was much greater than that of the air still trapped inside. If the *Bismarck* had sunk before the flooding of all her watertight compartments was virtually complete, this pressure differential would surely have led to cave-ins, causing her to look something like the *Titanic*'s stern, despite the stoutness of the battleship's construction. Instead we found a hull that appears whole and relatively undamaged by the descent and impact. The *Bismarck* did not implode."[32]

Although Ballard kept the location of the wreck secret to protect it from further disturbance, it was located by further expeditions in 2001–2002 and 2005 which carried out extensive filming. The second expedition also located the wreck of HMS *Hood*.[33] The wreckage of *Hood*, ripped into three sections by the explosion that destroyed the vessel, was consistent with the theory that an explosion in the aft magazines had destroyed the ship, but it also pointed to a second explosion that broke the for'ard remains of the ship in two. Analysis of the wreck of *Bismarck* by all teams found further evidence to support the idea that she had been scuttled. In particular, James Cameron's 2002 expedition was able to show evidence that the torpedoes which had struck *Bismarck* had not penetrated the inner core of the ship.

The remains of *Bismarck* lie some 600 miles west of Brest at a depth of 15,700 feet. Such is the slow decay of the vessel that it is estimated that she will continue to stand as a monument to the fate of so many of her crew well into the 22nd century. On the ocean bed around the wreck are hundreds of pairs of seamen's boots – a final ghostly reminder of the men who once filled them.

The Battle Summary charts the operations of the Royal Navy against Battleship *Bismarck*. There was much that the writers of the summary could not know. The summary was pulled together in some haste as the officers of the Royal Navy struggled to learn lessons for the future from recently concluded operations. The German perspective on these operations would not emerge until after 1945. With so few survivors from *Bismarck*, the final hours in the life of the battleship, especially the decisions taken by those on the bridge, remain beyond the reach of historians. Included here are first-hand accounts by survivors, both British and German, sourced from within the pages of the Hitler Conferences and separately from private, independent sources. Even the discovery of the wreck has not conclusively settled the issue of how the battleship sank.

Seventy years on from the events it analyses, the Battle Summary of the pursuit and sinking of *Bismarck* makes interesting reading, particularly here with the addition of specially selected sections of the minutes of the Conference of the Commander-in-Chief, Navy with the Führer at the Berghof on 22 May 1941.

References

1.   'The *Bismarck* Launched', *The Times*, 15 February 1939, p.11.
2.   Editorial, *The Times*, 15 February 1939, p.11.
3.   See for example, Brower, J. (2005), *The Battleship Bismarck (Anatomy of the Ship)*, Conway Maritime Press, London. Bercuson, D. J. & Herwig, H. H. (2003), *The Destruction of the Bismarck*, The Overlook Press, New York. Berthold, W. (1958), *The Sinking of The Bismarck*, Longmans, Green and Co., London. Busch, F. O. (1950), *Das Geheimnis der Bismarck*, Adolf Sponholtz Verlag, Hannover. Elfrath, U. & Herzog, B. (1989), *The Battleship Bismarck: A Documentary in Words and Pictures*, Schiffer Publishing, Atglen. Forester, C. S. (1959), *Hunting the Bismarck*, Amereon Ltd, London. Russell Grenfell, R. (1948), *The Bismarck Episode*, Faber and Faber, London. Jackson, R. (2002), *The Bismarck, Weapons of War*, London. Koop, G. & Schmolke, K-P. (1998), *Battleships of the Bismarck Class: Bismarck and Tirpitz: Culmination and Finale of German Battleship Construction*, Naval Institute Press, Annapolis. Rhys-Jones, G. (1999), *The Loss of the Bismarck: An Avoidable Disaster*, Cassell, London. McMurtrie, F. (1941), *The Cruise of the Bismarck*, Hutchinson & Co., London. Moffat, J. (2009), *I Sank the Bismarck*, Bantam Press, London. Schofield, B. B. (1972), *The Loss of the Bismarck*, Ian Allan, London. Shirer, W. L. (1962), *The Sinking of The Bismarck*, Random House, London. Winklareth, R. L. (1998), *The Bismarck Chase: New Light on a Famous Engagement*, Naval Institute Press, Annapolis. Zetterling, N. & Tamelander, M. (2009), *Bismarck: The Final Days of Germany's Greatest Battleship*, Casemate, Drexel Hill.
4.   Mulligan, T. P. (2005), Ship-of-the-Line or Atlantic Raider? Battleship *Bismarck* Between Design Limitations and Naval Strategy, *The Journal of Military History*, vol. 69 (October 2005), pp.1013–44.
5.   Bennett, G. H. & Bennett, R. (2004), *Hitler's Admirals*, United States Naval Institute Press, Annapolis. p.100.
6.   Bennett, G. H. & Bennett, R. (2004), *Hitler's Admirals*, United States Naval Institute Press, Annapolis. p.99.
7.   Admiral Assmann's report on the *Bismarck* operation June 1941, reproduced in Showell, J. P. M. (1990), *Führer Conferences on Naval Affairs 1939–1945*, Greenhill Books, London. pp.217–218.
8.   Admiral Assmann's report on the *Bismarck* operation June 1941, reproduced in Showell, J. P. M. (1990), *Führer Conferences on Naval Affairs 1939–1945*, Greenhill Books, London. p.204.
9.   Sopocko, E. (1942), *Gentlemen the Bismarck has been Sunk*, Methuen, London, 1942. p.51.
10. 'I was There! – I saw One Vast Explosion – the *Hood* had Gone', *The War Illustrated*, vol. 4, No.94, 20 June 1941. p.621.
11. On the loss of HMS *Hood* see the Board of Enquiry hearings and report, British National Archives (hereinafter TNA:PRO) ADM116/4351-4352.
12. On the actions of HMS *Prince of Wales* see TNA:PRO ADM 267/111.
13. Bennett, G. H. & Bennett, R. (2004), *Hitler's Admirals*, United States Naval Institute Press, Annapolis. p.101.

14. For an older account of this episode see Kennedy, L. (1991), *Pursuit: The sinking of the Bismarck*, Fontana London.
15. Willmot, H. P., (2002), *Battleship*, Cassell, London. p.163.
16. Un-named officer onboard HMS *King George V*, *The War Illustrated*, vol. 4, No.95, 27 June 1941. p.630.
17. Sopocko, E. (1942), *Gentlemen the Bismarck has been Sunk*, Methuen, London, 1942. p.83.
18. '*Bismarck* Epic', *The News Review*, 5 June 1941, p.12. '*Bismarck* Sunk', *San Francisco Chronicle*, 27 May 1941. p.1. '*Bismarck* Sunk', *New York Post*, 27 May 1941. p.1.
19. Von Below, N. (2010), *At Hitler's Side: The Memoirs of Hitler's Luftwaffe Adjutant 1937–1945*, Frontline Books, Barnsley. p.101.
20. John Deane Potter, Fiasco: *The Break-out of the German Battleships*, Reader's Union, London, 1970. pp.5–6.
21. Cajus Bekker, Verdammte See, Verlag Ullstein, Berlin, 1971. pp.216–217. Minutes of the Führer Conference on Naval Affairs, 6 June 1941, Jak P. Mallmann Showell, *Führer Conferences on Naval Affairs 1939–1945*, Greenhill Books, London, 1990. pp.217–218.
22. In addition there was considerable concern in the Admiralty and Foreign Office that the Japanese were providing assistance to German commerce raiders and blockade runners. See TNA:PRO FO371/28814.
23. Reproduced in Winston S. Churchill, *The Second World War*, vol. 3, The Reprint Society, London, 1952. p.259.
24. Reproduced in Winston S. Churchill, *The Second World War*, vol. 3, The Reprint Society, London, 1952. p.259.
25. See W.A. Marshall for the Lord's Commissioners of the Admiralty to the Undersecretary of State at the Air Ministry, 29 May 1946, TNA:PRO AIR15/204.
26. See proposed amendments to Commander-in-Chief Home Fleet's Despatch on the Sinking of the German Battleship *Bismarck* on 27 May 1941, TNA: PRO AIR15/204. See also further correspondence in TNA:PRO ADM1/19999.
27. Preliminary Report on Interrogation of Survivors of the German Battleship *Bismarck* sunk on 27 May 1941, British National Archives TNA: PRO ADM267/137.
28. Un-named officer on-board HMS *King George V*, *The War Illustrated*, vol. 4, No.95, 27 June 1941. p.630.
29. Survivor's Report by Ordinary Seaman Herbert Manthey contained in Showell, J. P. M. (1990), *Führer Conferences on Naval Affairs 1939–1945*, Greenhill Books, London. p.216. See also the account by *Bismarck*'s senior surviving officer von Mullenheim-Rechberg, B. (1980), *Battleship Bismarck, A Survivor's Story*, Naval Institute Press, Annapolis.
30. Rear-Admiral Beamish in debate on the 1942 Naval Estimates, House of Commons Debates, 26 February 1942, vol. 378, cols. 402–403.
31. Ballard, R. D. (1990), *Bismarck: Germany's Greatest Battleship Gives Up its Secrets*, Madison Publishing, Toronto.
32. Ballard, R. D. (1990) *The Discovery of the Bismarck*, Guild Publishing, London. pp.214–215.
33. Mearns, D. & White, R. (2001) *Hood and Bismarck. The Deep-Sea Discovery of an Epic Battle*, Channel 4 Books, London.

We are indebted to Martyn Anderson for his help in researching and preparing the books in this series for publication.

Part I

The collection of documents known as the "Führer Conferences" was among the German Naval Archives captured by British and American Intelligence Officers at Tambach during the war.

The "Führer Conferences" are minutes of staff meetings between Hitler and the various commanders of the German Forces. Those presented here relate to naval affairs, and were written up from rough notes taken by the Commander-in-Chief, Navy or his deputy during the conferences.

The minutes are often verbose and filled with minor technical details. These minor details have either been summarised or omitted so as to bring out clearly the main Naval problems confronting Germany and how these problems were dealt with by a totalitarian state.

The German account of this action is given in the following reports and signals taken from the German Naval Archives.

Führer Conferences on Naval Affairs, 1941

Report of the Commander-in-Chief, Navy to the Führer on 20 April 1941

1. German operational situation:

Important points in present naval strategy:

    a. Cruiser warfare in foreign waters.

    b. Submarine warfare.

    c. Protection of all transport and convoy traffic to Norway and in the North Sea and Western Area.

Re a: Cruiser warfare is still successful, though restricted to a certain extent by necessary overhauling and replenishment of supplies. At present five auxiliary cruisers are still operating. Ship "10" is on return passage in the North Atlantic.

Ship "41", operating in the Atlantic, has reported sinking 56, 000 tons since the middle of December 1940. Apart from this, one other auxiliary cruiser is in the South Atlantic, two are in the western Indian Ocean, and one is in the eastern Indian Ocean.

The numerous supply ships engaged in replenishing the supplies of auxiliary cruisers and submarines in the Indian and South Atlantic Oceans have hitherto been remarkably successful. Only one prize tanker was lost. At the moment three prize ships are en route to Germany.

Re b: The northern submarine operational area is being shifted from the region just outside the North Channel to an area farther west, southwest of Iceland, on account of enemy patrols and the short, bright nights.

The number of submarines is gradually increasing. At present there are only thirty operational boats. Taking losses into account, the probable number of operational boats will be as follows: On 1 May, 37; on 1 June, 39; on 1 July, 43; and on 1 August, 52.

Re c: In spite of increased enemy efforts to stop or disrupt transport traffic by air attacks, transports to Oslo have continued without interruption. Losses on the west coast of Norway and in the North Sea and the Channel have been satisfactorily small up to now. This shows the effectiveness of the anti-aircraft guns onboard patrol vessels and mine sweepers!!

The next operation with battleships *Bismarck* and *Prinz Eugen* is scheduled for the end of April, when the ships are to leave home waters for the Atlantic.

The questions of anti-aircraft defences for the base at Brest, bomb and torpedo hits on the *Gneisenau*, and bases on the west coast of France are discussed.

The Commander-in-Chief, Navy points out that the danger to ships under repair in Kiel and Wilhelmshaven is as great at present as it is in Brest, apart from the fact that a single plane can carry a greater bomb load to Brest. In spite of this, until further notice large ships will put into Brest only in exceptional circumstances. The occupation of Ferrol, which the Führer is determined to carry out in the autumn, is of great importance. If possible the Führer would like to see the Todt Organization quickly construct a large dry dock in Trondheim. This is being investigated.

2. Intensification of the use of aerial mines:

A new firing device for aerial mines, combining magnetic and acoustic firing, will be ready in May. It is necessary to employ this new firing method at once and as extensively as possible before the enemy discovers the new principle and develops appropriate methods for sweeping the mines. In view of previous firing devices, a conjecture concerning the combination of the new firing device is comparatively easy, even for the enemy. In connection with the mining of the Suez Canal, a new combination of this sort was supposedly already suspected.

The mining of the Suez Canal, together with the threat to the British lines of communication through the Straits of Sicily by the X Air Corps, is a classic example of a practical mining operation which has achieved the desired strategic effect – by being executed at precisely the right moment. Perseverance in laying the mines and patience in giving them time to take effect are necessary conditions for success.

Continual use of aerial mines at the entrance of harbours is the most effective way of supplementing operations by submarines, surface forces, and aircraft against British supply lines.

Considering that our mines present a grave threat to the enemy, while his countermeasures have reached a high degree of efficiency as the result of one and a half years of wartime experience, it is evident that the outcome of the race between offensive mine warfare and anti-mine defence will be of decisive importance. Offensive mine warfare has the advantage at this time, in view of the new firing device with which our mines will be equipped in the near future. However, it is certain that this advantage will prevail for a limited time only. It is therefore imperative that it be exploited at once to the fullest possible extent. Therefore both the Air Force and the Navy must lay aerial mines in large numbers immediately. The Führer will see to it that the Air Force acts accordingly.

3. The question of sending German submarines to the Mediterranean:

The present situation in the Mediterranean seems to indicate that operations by German submarines against British transport traffic in the eastern Mediterranean would be particularly desirable and promising. In addition to sinking ships, they would have a strategic effect on Army operations ashore! A detailed examination of the question of sending submarines to the Mediterranean, however, has shown that the disadvantages of doing this probably outweigh possible advantages. The suggestion is therefore to be disregarded.

Reasons:

   a. The main objective of submarine warfare remains the attack on imports to the British Isles. The concentration of supply ships into convoys demands a similar concentration of the attacking forces, especially as sufficient reconnaissance is lacking owing to the fact that air reconnaissance cannot operate as far out as the submarine operational area. At present only thirty operational boats are available, including those being over-hauled. About half of this number are at sea, counting submarines either outward or homeward bound; therefore only one third, or ten, are in the operational area. This small number is sufficient for locating and attacking an occasional convoy in the two main operational areas west of Britain and west of Africa. Any division of forces necessarily reduces the chances for intercepting and destroying convoys.

b. For operations in the Mediterranean only small boats manned by experienced crews can be considered, in view of the conditions under which they would have to operate. The approach route is very long, and the first boat would not be available in the Aegean or the eastern Mediterranean before 7 May at the earliest; additional boats not until the middle of May.

c. The effect of single submarines would be very small. At present overhaul and repair is possible only in Italy, which means that boats would have to return to an Italian port after every ten days or two weeks of operations, involving a long voyage to and from the operational area. Really promising operations would therefore be possible only with at least ten boats. This would mean, however, that submarine warfare against the main target, British imports, would be weakened decidedly.

d. The establishment of an Italian base for our submarines, or a suitable base in Yugoslavia or Greece would require at least four weeks of preparation for installation of necessary workshops, provision of technicians and base personnel, supplies, etc. This would necessarily weaken our submarine bases in Germany and in the Atlantic.

e. The clear water and the necessity of remaining submerged for prolonged periods make the situation in the Mediterranean unfavourable for submarine warfare. For this reason alone single boats would not accomplish much.

In summary, the Naval Staff considers that the prospects of success for single boats do not compensate for the disadvantages ensuing from removing them from the main theatre of operations in the Atlantic. It is therefore proposed, as already reported, to withdraw Italian submarines from the Atlantic and to concentrate a strong force of Italian submarines in the eastern Mediterranean.

The present is a good time for the withdrawal, since the Italians must realize that their submarines are badly needed in the eastern Mediterranean.

The Führer is in complete agreement with the decision not to send German submarines into the Mediterranean, likewise with the withdrawal of Italian submarines from the Atlantic.

4. Restrictions on naval warfare as the result of the Pan-American Safety Zone:

In the presence of the German Foreign Minister the Führer decides as follows: In view of America's present undecided attitude resulting from events in the Balkans, the zone as far as 20° N (that part which is off the U.S. coast) will for the present be recognized, but further south only a 300 mile zone, No note is to be sent to the U.S.A., etc.

5. Sanction for warfare against merchant ships of the U.S.A. according to prize regulations:

For the same reason as stated under "4", the following procedure is to be used:

For from ten days to two weeks there is to be no change; however, the *Bismarck* and the *Prinz Eugen* can receive instructions for action, which can be put into force by means of a code word, as soon as the Führer has decided accordingly.

The Foreign Minister states that he agreed to attacks on neutral ships proceeding alone in the new closed area only providing they are doing escort duty for merchant ships. (According to the definite instructions received from the Armed Forces High Command, unrestricted offensive action was sanctioned against all naval and merchant vessels in the blockade area.)

6. Relations with Japan:

What were the results of Matsuoka's visit? Was operation 'Barbarossa' mentioned during the conference? What views are held with regard to the Russo-Japanese pact?

The Führer answers that Matsuoka was informed that Russia will not be attacked as long as she maintains a friendly attitude in accordance with the treaty; if this is not the case, he reserves the right to take suitable action. The Russo-Japanese pact was concluded with Germany's acquiescence. The above stand taken by the Führer has had a salutary effect on the attitude of Russia, who will now conduct herself with great correctness and who expects no attack for the present.

The Führer values the Russo-Japanese pact because Japan is now restrained from taking action against Vladivostok and should be induced to attack Singapore instead. Matsuoka and Oshima have assured him that all preparations will be completed by May.

The Commander-in-Chief, Navy draws attention to the extremely vague and non-committal statements of Nomura; he intends to continue to try to influence him.

7. Relations with Russia:
   What is the Führer's opinion of the present change in Russia's attitude in an obviously pro-German direction?

   The Führer replies in the same vein as under Paragraph 6.

   The Commander-in-Chief, Navy points out the need for taking effective steps to mine the White Sea Canal so that submarines and destroyers cannot escape into the Arctic Ocean, and the urgent necessity for heavy air bombardment of the locks in the canal, as it is of little use to mine the Neva.

   The Führer agrees.

8. Conferences between the Army General Staff and the Finnish General Staff have already begun. When can the naval conferences be expected to begin?

   The Führer replies that the conferences so far have been of a very general nature. The time for naval conferences has not yet arrived. Nevertheless the Führer fully realizes the importance of this matter.

9. Relations with France:
   Does the Führer still consider operation 'Attila' necessary?

   The Führer replies that it must be held in readiness for the present, even though he is inclined to believe that Darlan's attitude is trustworthy.

10. Italo-German co-operation in the Aegean Sea:
    The following arrangements have been agreed upon:
    a. Territorial limits. The east coast of Greece, including the Gulf of Athens, comes under the command of the Admiral, Southeast; also the islands off the coast and the islands in the Aegean Sea, as far as they are occupied by German troops. The Peloponnesus and the west coast of Greece come under the command of Italy.
    b. Enlistment of Italian naval forces for duty along the German coastal sector for the defence of harbours and inshore waters and as escorts for coastal traffic and island transports. Request has been made for two torpedo boat or destroyer flotillas of

four ships each, three mine-sweeping and three patrol flotillas of six vessels each, two subchaser flotillas, two or three PT boat flotillas of eight boats each, six mine layers, and six submarines, as well as several small transports, tankers, and other supply ships. The Italian Naval Staff has agreed to provide these vessels, but has pointed out that all available submarines are at present engaged in operations against British transports in the eastern Mediterranean. Apart from the forces applied for, the Italian Naval Staff plans to put Italian forces stationed permanently or temporarily in the Dodecanese Islands at the disposal of the Admiral, Southeast, should he require them.

c. Liaison between Italian naval forces and the Admiral, Southeast. An Italian Chief of Staff, who will also be the commander of the above Italian naval forces, will be attached to the Admiral, Southeast. The Admiral, Southeast is permitted to transfer sections of these forces to commanders subordinate to him. The Dodecanese naval forces temporarily placed at the disposal of the Admiral, Southeast will be operationally and tactically under his command during this time.

Captain Count Peccori-Giraldi has been selected as Chief of Staff.

(Signed) Raeder.

In Greece the Allied situation deteriorated and on 21 April the Greek Government informed Britain of their inability to resist further and asked the British forces to withdraw. Evacuation began on 22 April, and by 26 April the Germans had captured the Isthmus and town of Korinth, entering Athens on the following day. British forces rallied in Crete, and the Germans began preparing a parachute operation against the island – operation 'Merkur'. Goering was placed in command of the operation, and the naval share was limited to transport operations from Greece as soon as Crete had been taken.

The attack on Crete began on the morning of 20 May. The attack was in the beginning entirely by air, and the air defences of the island which had been previously reduced to 7 serviceable aircraft were overwhelmed. Ships of the Royal Navy which were disposed for the defence of the island suffered heavily from German air attacks, but managed to destroy the few German transports which attempted to land troops on the island. Air attacks intensified and prevented ships from operating in the vicinity of Crete by day, but night actions were continued regardless of the opposition. British troops, when the action began, had only recently been evacuated from Greece. They were ill-equipped and had little more than rifles and a few light automatics with which to defend the island. Naval vessels had brought in additional supplies, but by 27 May the situation was hopeless, and evacuation began. It was completed by 1 June.

Further exploitation of the situation in the Eastern Mediterranean was envisaged in the following directive from Hitler:

Führer and Supreme Commander   Führer Headquarters
of the Wehrmacht.   25.5.1941

Top Secret
Führer Directive No. 30 – Middle East

1. The Arabian Freedom Movement is our natural ally in the Middle East against England. In this connection the rebellion in Iraq assumes a special importance. Its influence extends beyond the boundaries of Iraq and strengthens anti-British forces in the Middle East, it disturbs British communications and ties down British troops and shipping at the expense of other theatres of war.

   I have decided therefore, to encourage developments in the Middle East by supporting Iraq.

   Whether – and if so by what means – it would be possible afterwards to launch an offensive against the Suez Canal and eventually oust the British finally from their position between the Mediterranean and the Persian Gulf cannot be decided until operation 'Barbarossa' is complete

2. My decisions for the support of Iraq can be summarized as follows:

   The sending of a Military Mission

   Assistance from the Luftwaffe

   The supply of arms.

3. The Military Mission will be commanded by General der Flieger Felmy. (Its code name will be Special Staff F). Its tasks are:

   a. to advise and support the armed forces of Iraq.

   b. to establish as far as possible military liaison with anti-British forces, including those outside Iraq.

c. to gain experience and information from this area for the German Wehrmacht.

The composition of the mission in view of these tasks will be in the hands of the Chief of the Armed Forces Supreme Command. The Chain of Command is as follows:

a. The Head of the Military Mission is in command of all members of the Wehrmacht sent to Iraq as well as the Syria Liaison Detachment.

b. The Head of the Military Mission is subordinate to the Chief of the Armed Forces Supreme Command with the proviso that orders and directives for air units shall be issued exclusively by the C. in C. of the Luftwaffe.

c. The Head of the Military Mission will have dealings with military offices only in Iraq. Matters concerning the Mission which require negotiations with the Iraq Government will be handled by the Foreign Office representative in Iraq.

Before any military orders are given which may have repercussions on foreign policy the Head of the Military Mission must obtain the consent of the Foreign Office representative in Iraq.

d. For the present the members of the Military Mission are to be regarded as Volunteers (after the style of the Condor Legion). They will wear tropical uniform with Iraq badges. German aircraft also will show Iraq markings.

4. Luftwaffe

The numerical force of the Luftwaffe which should be employed is to be limited. Its function is not merely that of an arm of the Wehrmacht, but in addition it is that of an agent for prompting greater self-confidence and will to resist among the Iraq Armed Forces and civilians.

The nature and extent of German intervention is to be decided by the C. in C. of the Luftwaffe.

5. Supply of Arms

The necessary orders (deliveries from Syria by virtue of the agreement made with the French for this purpose; and from Germany) will be given by the Chief of the Supreme Command of the Armed Forces.

6. The Direction of Propaganda in the Middle East is the responsibility of the Foreign Office, working in this instance with the Supreme Command of the Armed Forces.

   The Basis of the Propaganda is:

   "An Axis victory will bring to the nations of the Middle East freedom from the British yoke and the right of self-determination. All lovers of freedom will therefore join in the fight against England."

   Anti-French propaganda in Syria must be suspended for the time being.

7. Where members of the Italian Armed Forces are employed in Iraq, it will be necessary to co-operate with them in accordance with this directive. Efforts are being made to bring them within the sphere of authority of the Head of the German Military Mission.

(Signed) Adolf Hitler.

Sinking of the Bismarck

The most important operation of the German Navy in May, 1941 was operation 'Rheinuebung' (Rhine Exercise). This operation was the climax of the series of naval attacks against merchant shipping in the Atlantic. For it the newly completed battleship *Bismarck* and the new heavy cruiser *Prinz Eugen* were to make a three month sortie in the Atlantic. Great results were expected and everything possible was done to make the operation a success. Tankers and reconnaissance merchant ships were placed in strategic positions, and an elaborate wireless intelligence organization was set up to track down convoys and independent merchant ships.

On 21 May the ships sailed, and on the following day Raeder reported to Hitler. There was, however, little discussion on the forthcoming operation.

Conference of the Commander-in-Chief, Navy with the Führer at the Berghof on 22 May 1941

Also present: **Chief of Staff, Armed Forces High Command**
General Jodl
Captain von Puttkamer
The Foreign Minister

1. Situation.
    a. Submarine warfare: Since the beginning of May there has been a further increase in the number of ships sunk by our submarines. Eleven boats are at present in the northern operational area and seven are in the southern area. In the course of the last few days about 85,000 tons were sunk from a convoy. The enemy had adopted a very flexible convoy system, combined with a far-reaching and excellent direction-finding and locator network; the sighting and location reports are evaluated very rapidly for the purpose of convoy control. Enemy defence for convoys has been considerably strengthened; a close watch of the sea area west of Britain is being kept by air reconnaissance, anti-submarine groups, surface forces, and single steamers. The losses incurred by us in March and April made it necessary to move the submarines further out into the Atlantic. Some of the waiting positions are outside the declared blockade area. Successful submarine operations have been carried out in the area

off the West African coast near Freetown. One boat has set out on a mine-laying mission in the Takoradi-Lagos area.

b. Cruiser warfare in foreign waters: Four auxiliary cruisers are still on operations, one in the South Atlantic and three in the Indian Ocean. Ship "10", commanded by Captain Kaehler, returned to Hamburg after nearly eleven months of operations. The ship sank 96,000 tons. Engagements were fought with three superior enemy auxiliary cruisers, one of which was sunk and the other two badly damaged.

Ship "33", commanded by Captain Krueder, sank at noon on 8 May in the Indian Ocean west of Somaliland during an engagement with the heavy British cruiser *Cornwall*, which has eight 20.3-cm. guns. Only fifty three survivors were taken prisoner. The enemy himself reported damage to the *Cornwall* during the engagement.

The Commanding Officer's character is a sufficient guarantee that the auxiliary cruiser fought a gallant battle after vainly attempting to escape from the enemy cruiser through use of deception. Ship "33" was the most successful German auxiliary cruiser, which carried out extremely well all the tactical and operational demands made of her.

Her successes amounted to 120,000 tons, including several prizes brought to home waters amounting to over 50,000 tons. Three large whale ships from the Antarctic, carrying 22,000 tons of whale oil, were among the prizes; also eight smaller whalers, a valuable tanker, and a steamer carrying wheat. At least two further ships, the names of which are unknown, were captured before the engagement with the *Cornwall*. Mine-laying missions in Australian waters were brilliantly executed. Apart from sinkings directly caused by the mines (three to four steamers and one mine sweeper have been sunk as far as is known at present), these mine operations have great operational effect with extremely far-reaching consequences for enemy shipping. The total success achieved by ship "33" exceeds that of cruiser *Emden* or auxiliary cruiser *Wolf* in the World War.

Proposal: These facts, together with the name of this outstanding commanding officer, should be mentioned and given recognition in one of the next reports of the Armed Forces High Command.

The Führer agrees. He also agrees to announcing the loss of Lt. Comdr. Prien at a time when substantial submarine successes are reported.

The prize *Speybank* put into Bordeaux on 11 May with a very valuable cargo of 1,500 tons of manganese, 300 tons of rubber, jute, and tea.

The supply ship *Dresden* put into a harbour in southern France with 140 Americans, some of them women and children, who were taken aboard auxiliary cruisers during the capture of an Egyptian steamer. It is inexcusable of the U.S. Government to allow American citizens, including women and children, to travel on ships belonging to belligerents.

The captain of the *Dresden* treated the American passengers with great consideration, so that no protests are likely.

c. Warfare by surface forces against merchant shipping: The *Bismarck-Prinz Eugen* task force is en route to its mission in the Atlantic; the ships left Norwegian waters near Bergen on 21 May. The purpose of the operation is war against merchant shipping in the North and Middle Atlantic. Fleet Commander Admiral Luetjens is in command of the operation.

d. German merchant shipping overseas: Of the four blockade-runners sent to South America, the first is on the return voyage and will arrive at the end of May; the remaining three are discharging and taking on cargo in Brazil. Up to now goods valued at 19,000,000 reichsmark have been exported.

Two German merchant ships, carrying 7,000 tons of rubber in all, are at present en route from Mairen. In a few days a third one will follow with an additional 4,000 tons. The first vessel is to arrive about the end of June; she will proceed by way of Cape Horn.

Five vessels put out from Chile for Japan.

2. The enemy's air forces are very active in attacking German convoy and coastal traffic on the Norwegian and German coasts and the occupied Channel coast. Up to now the enemy has achieved no great success, and our defence forces have had good results in shooting down aircraft.

3. Extension of inland waterways in Holland.

The Navy is very much interested in developing the inland waterways from the Ems River and the city of Delfzijl to Amsterdam, Rotterdam and the Rhine River in order to reduce traffic on the sea route, which is exposed to great danger from air attacks, motor-boats, and mines, and in order to economize in the use of our limited escort forces. The Navy has ascertained that it is altogether possible to increase the number of barges on the canals and to utilize them better. Even partial expansion would mean a substantial increase in the amounts transported and would be of advantage to the over-all conduct of the war, not to mention its great importance for peacetime purposes. Up to now the Ministry of Transport has opposed this project. The Naval Staff cannot judge the reasons for this. It is proposed that the Führer should recommend this expansion.

The Chief of Staff, Armed Forces High Command will attend to the matter.

4. Continuing use of aerial mines.

In view of the importance of our new mine fuse and the necessity for exploiting it to the fullest possible extent before the enemy counter-measures become effective, the Naval Staff has recommended mine-laying operations on a large scale to the Commander-in-Chief, Air. (A copy of the suggestion was sent to the Armed Forces High Command.)

As far as is known the Operations Staff of the Commander-in-Chief, Air agrees in principle with the views of the Naval Staff, but considers that the number of aircraft available would not be sufficient for large-scale operations because of the withdrawal of large forces for the Eastern Campaign.

General Jodl states that the Air Force has agreed to undertake a large-scale mine-laying operation with all available aircraft.

5. Discussion of the present problem of naval warfare in the Atlantic due to the attitude of the U.S.A.

6. Possible exploitation of French bases in West Africa.

The Chief of Staff, Armed Forces High Command states that there are prospects that the French will agree to all our demands. The French have made far-reaching preparations for defending Northwest Africa against British and American attacks.

7. Canary Islands. Spanish Navy:

    a. The Commander-in-Chief, Navy recommends speedy measures for reinforcing the defences of the Canaries so that the islands can be held at any time against the British and Americans. Such measures would include exporting and installing 15-cm. guns and building up supplies of food and ammunition. Enemy occupation of the Canary Islands would endanger our position in West Africa.

The Führer agrees that the Armed Forces High Command should make preparations for these measures and that they should be carried out.

b. During negotiations between the German and Spanish Navies regarding equipment for Spain, agreement was reached on most points; e.g., German mines are to be delivered. This could be done at once and would be in the interest of the German Navy. Delivery is being delayed, however, by trivial bickering on the part of the Ministry of Economics. The Commander-in-Chief, Navy requests that the Foreign Office clarify the matter.

The Foreign Minister will attend to the matter.

8. Occupation of the Azores.

This subject was brought up by the Führer. Judging from an earlier summary of the situation, which has not undergone any changes since, it would be possible to carry out the initial occupation of the Azores, using combat forces. It is extremely unlikely, however, that the islands could be held and supplies brought up in the face of British, possibly also American attacks. Moreover, all our combat forces, including submarines, would be necessary to achieve this, and they would therefore have to be withdrawn from all offensive activities in the Battle of the Atlantic; this is intolerable. The Navy must therefore reject the idea of occupying the Azores.

The Führer is still in favour of occupying the Azores, in order to be able to operate long-range bombers from there against the U.S.A. The occasion for this may arise by autumn. In reply to the Commander-in-Chief, Navy, the Führer confirms that the Navy's main task in summer 1941 must be the disruption of British supply lines.

9. Plans for operation 'Barbarossa':

It is essential that contact and conferences with the Finnish Admiralty be approved soon, at least as regards negotiations on fundamental operational matters, the settlement of which must be considered an essential factor for any operations. Such conferences require lengthy preparation; questions to be discussed include fuel supplies, anti-aircraft defence of bases and anchorages, supplies of foodstuffs, prompt transfer of vessels from the shipyards, etc.

The Chief of Staff, Armed Forces High Command states that following the return of Minister Schnurre within the next few days, negotiations will take place between the Armed Forces High Command and the Finns. Subsequently, discussions on the part of the Navy will be possible.

Transports to Finland will, as ordered, be carried out in ten instead of twenty one days. Twenty five steamers will be withdrawn from merchant shipping for this purpose.

10. Organization in the southeastern area:

According to Führer Directive No. 29, it is intended that the Army shall hand over the defence of the whole Greek area, up to Salonika, to the Italian Armed Forces after completion of operation 'Merkur'. The directive leaves open for later settlement the question of who is ultimately to provide the occupational forces for Crete. Attention is called to the decisive importance of defending the main strategic points such as Salonika, Lemnos, Piraeus, Melos, and Crete. These points are of decisive importance as strategic bases for any further operations in the Eastern Mediterranean. It is essential that they be adequately protected against all eventualities and be ready to offer determined resistance to any enemy action. This is a necessary condition for successful operations by the X Air Corps. Such protection, however, can be guaranteed only if coastal defence and occupation of the hinterland is in the hands of German forces. The Naval Staff is therefore of the opinion that the bases in question should be firmly held by German forces until the Mediterranean operation as a whole has been concluded, more specifically, until British operations in the Eastern Mediterranean, including Alexandria and the Suez, have been eliminated. This applies especially to Crete, which is essential to the X Air Corps.

The Führer agrees, and gives the Chief of Staff, Armed Forces High Command appropriate instructions.

11. Italian submarines:

The Commander-in-Chief, Navy once again requests withdrawal of Italian submarines from the Atlantic. The time is propitious, since they are urgently needed in the Eastern Mediterranean.

The Foreign Minister proposes that he raise this point with Count Ciano or that the Führer discuss it at his next meeting with the Duce, which is to take place soon.

The Führer agrees.

12. The Commander-in-Chief, Navy asks the Führer for his opinion on Japan's attitude, as he is under the impression that the Japanese are rather cool. (Nomura is negotiating in Washington!)

At the present time the Führer has no clear picture of the situation but obviously there are internal political difficulties in Japan. The good friendship policy is to be continued.

The Commander-in-Chief, Navy reports on information received from Admiral Nomura regarding new ships built by the Japanese.

The Führer emphasizes the necessity for complete secrecy.

13. The Commander-in-Chief, Navy stresses the need for deepening navigational channels to accommodate very heavy new vessels after the war. The depth of the Kiel Canal, the Belts, and Jade Bay should be increased to fifteen metres. This work is to be carried out by the Navy, while the Elbe and Weser Rivers should be deepened as a large-scale project of other governmental agencies.

The Führer agrees entirely, but points out also the urgency of expanding Trondheim.

14. The Commander-in-Chief, Navy states that very careful and detailed preparations have been made for holding back the important materials to be delivered to Russia. The Russian Navy will be informed in the near future that the German Navy is having to draw on some of the things in view of the state of emergency, so that slight delays will occur, but that deliveries as a whole are not jeopardized.

The Führer agrees. The Foreign Minister has been informed.

15. The Commander-in-Chief, Navy reports that it will take eight months to complete constructing the aircraft carrier, including installations of anti-aircraft guns, if the work is resumed at the conclusion of operation 'Barbarossa'. An additional year will be needed for trials. As soon as it

has definitely been decided to continue work on the carrier, the Führer should order the Commander-in-Chief, Air to make the necessary planes available in time.

(Signed) Raeder

Part II

C.B. 3081 (3)   Restricted

NAVAL STAFF HISTORY
SECOND WORLD WAR

BATTLE SUMMARY No. 5

THE CHASE AND SINKING OF THE GERMAN BATTLESHIP BISMARCK
May 23–27, 1941

T.S.D. 307/42
Training and Staff Duties Division (Historical Section),
Naval Staff, Admiralty, S.W.1

CONTENTS

Appendices

The *Bismarck* Sails

In the battle for the seas, raiders and aircraft have played an important part, roughly one half of the shipping losses being due to submarines and the remainder to raiders and aircraft.[1] Their principal field of attack has been the Atlantic and it was to the Atlantic that the cruiser *Prinz Eugen* and the *Bismarck*, the newest and finest battleship in the German Navy, took their way in May. The *Bismarck* was commanded by Captain Ernst Lindemann and flew the flag of Admiral Gunther Lütjens. She carried no less than 2,300 persons. Her main armament consisted of 8 38-cm. (15-in.) mounted in pairs in four centre line turrets. Her secondary armament was 12 15-cm. (5.9-in.) in pairs in turrets on each side of the upper deck. She had 16 10.5-cm. (4.1-in.) and a number of smaller guns. She could steam 27 knots. "You are the pride of the Navy", said Hitler when he visited her in May. She left Gothenhafen, near Kiel, on 19 May, to launch a big and concerted attack on British trade in the Atlantic.

Führer Conferences on Naval Affairs 1941

Besides achieving considerable tactical successes, the first operation of battleships *Gneisenau* and *Scharnhorst* in the Atlantic from January to March 1941 and the operation of cruiser *Hipper*, confirmed the fact that such use of surface vessels has far-reaching strategic effects. These effects were not restricted to the waters chosen as the zone of operations, but extended in widely diverging directions to other theatres of war, that is, also to the Mediterranean and the South Atlantic.

Hence naval warfare had to attempt to preserve and intensify the effects of the initial operations by repeating similar operations as frequently as possible, making the most of the experiences gained. In view of the decisive significance which British supplies in the North Atlantic have for the outcome of the war, German naval warfare can most effectively achieve its object only in the North Atlantic.

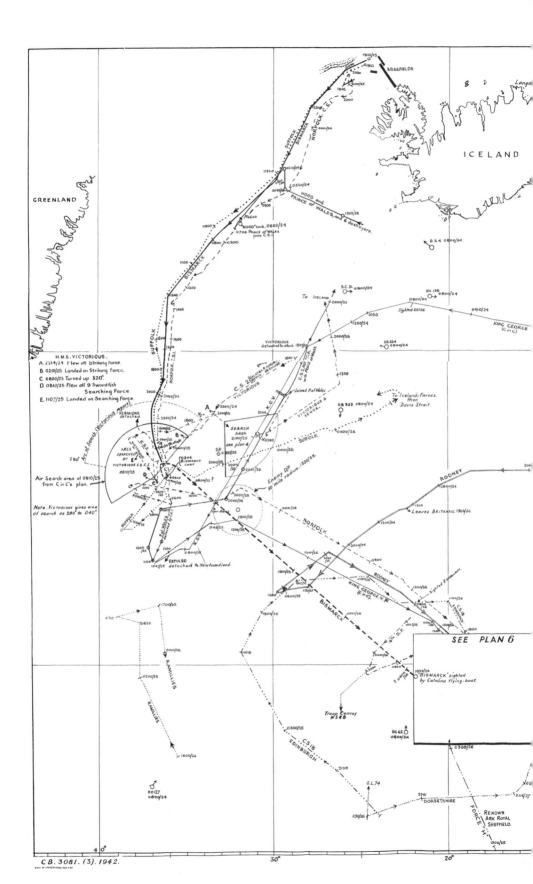

GREENLAND

ICELAND

MINEFIELDS

Langa

B D

H.M.S. VICTORIOUS.
A. 2214/24 Flew off Striking Force.
B. 0201/25 Landed on Striking Force.
C. 0800/25 Turned up 320°.
D. 0810/25 Flew off 9 Swordfish
   Searching Force.
E. 1107/25 Landed on Searching Force.

Air Search area of 0810/25
from C in C's plan.

Note. Victorious gives area
of search as 280° to 040°.

HOOD and
PRINCE of WALES, and 6 destroyers.

HOOD sunk. 0600/24
0706 PRINCE of WALES
joins C.S.1.

SUFFOLK

NORFOLK. C.S.I.

BISMARCK

SUFFOLK

NORFOLK C.S.I.

D.S.4. 0800/24

To Iceland

VICTORIOUS
detached to attack 1507/25

C.S. 2 (GALATEA, AURORA,
KENYA, HERMIONE, NEPTUNE)
VICTORIOUS

S.C.31 0600/24

H.A.126 0800/24
Sighted RX726   0410/24

KING GEORGE
(C in C)

1050

0 B 324 0800/24

Joined Pr. of Wales

K.G.V.

VICTORIOUS &
KENYA

0 B 323 0800/24

To Iceland-Faroes,
then
Davis Strait.

HERMIONE
detached

SEARCH
AREA
2100/25
see plan 4

SUFFOLK

Enemy D/F
50 mile radius, 1320/26.

RODNEY

2000/24

Leaves Britannic 1300/24

AREA SEARCHED
BY VICTORIOUS &2 C.S.

0306
BISMARCK
LOST

NORFOLK

280°

REPULSE
1047/25 detached to Newfoundland.

Pr. WALES
K.G.V.

KING GEORGE.V. III
(C in C)

RODNEY

Sighted Enemy

C.S.18

1700/25

1130

R.AMILLIES

R.AMILLIES

SEE PLAN 6

BISMARCK

Troop Convoy
WS8B

1030/26
BISMARCK sighted
by Catalina flying-boat.

0300/26

H G 62
0800/26

C.S.18
EDINBURGH

S.L.74

RX127
0800/24

DORSETSHIRE

FORCE H

RENOWN
ARK ROYAL
SHEFFIELD.

1300/25

4°0'

30°

20°

BISMARCK OPERATIONS
MAY 23-26.
1941.

FirstReports

On 20 May two large warships, strongly escorted, were seen at 1500 steaming northward out of the Kattegat. The Naval Attaché[2] at Stockholm got the news and at 2100 that night sent it to the Admiralty. A reconnaissance plane flying over Bergen reported in one of the fjords[3] there at 1330/21 two *Hipper* class cruisers, one of which was later identified by its photograph as the *Bismarck*. The intelligence went out at once to the fleet.

Plan 1 (*for Plan 6, see pages 86–87*)

BRITANNIA NAVAL HISTORIES OF WORLD WAR II

First Dispositions

The Commander-in-Chief (Admiral Sir John Tovey) at Scapa in the *King George V* brought the *King George V* and the 2nd Cruiser Squadron Rear-Admiral A. T. Curteis (*Galatea*, *Aurora*, *Kenya* and *Neptune)*, to short notice. Rear-Admiral W. F. Wake-Walker, R.A. 1st Cruiser Squadron who was already in Denmark Strait[4] with the cruisers *Norfolk* and *Suffolk*, was told to continue his patrol. The battlecruiser *Hood* (Vice-Admiral L. E. Holland) with the new battleship *Prince of Wales* and six destroyers (*Electra*, *Anthony*, *Echo*, *Icarus*, *Achates*, and *Antelope)* was ordered to cover the *Norfolk's* patrol in Denmark Strait. They passed the Hoxa boom at 0050/22. The *Manchester* and *Birmingham* (12 6-in.) who were already patrolling between Iceland and Faroes, were ordered to fuel at Skaalefjord (Iceland) and resume their patrol.

The battlecruiser *Repulse* was at the Clyde and the aircraft carrier *Victorious* at Scapa, due to sail on 22 May with a troop convoy (WS8B for the Middle East). Their sailing was cancelled and they were placed at the disposal of the Commander-in-Chief. A bombing attack despatched to the Norwegian coast proved abortive. The coast was wrapt in fog, and only two aircraft succeeded in reaching the fjord. They saw nothing of the enemy. Such was the situation on 21 May. On 22 May the weather was worse. In the North Sea there was cloud down to 200 feet; in Denmark Strait aircraft reported unbroken cloud down to 300 feet with heavy continuous rain and a visibility of less than half a mile. The air patrols could see nothing. Everywhere there was fog and uncertainty. It was under these conditions that the Commanding Officer, Captain H. L. St. J. Fancourt, at Royal Naval Air Station, Hatston, Orkneys, sent on his own initiative a plane across the North Sea.[5] It entered the Bergen fjords, and, under heavy fire, forced home a skilful and determined reconnaissance. The ships were not there. The information reached the Commander-in-Chief at 2000/22. Where was the enemy bound? To Northern Norway or to Iceland or to attack the Atlantic trade routes? The Commander-in-Chief considered the last to be the greatest menace and took immediate steps to counter it.

The *Suffolk* was ordered to rejoin the *Norfolk* in Denmark Strait. The *Arethusa* was to join the *Manchester* and *Birmingham* to form a patrol line between Iceland and the Faroes. Vice-Admiral Holland, with the *Hood* and *Prince of Wales*, then on their way to Iceland, was told to cover the patrols in Denmark Strait, North of 62° N. The Commander-in-Chief would cover the passages south of 62° N. Air reconnaissance was arranged for Denmark Strait (180 miles), Iceland to Faroes (255 miles), Faroes to Shetlands (165 miles) and the Norwegian coast.

Meanwhile the *Bismarck* and *Prinz Eugen* had sailed at 1945/21; they passed Trondheim on 0700/22, proceeding north at 24 knots as far as 64°. At 2100/22 they were in 68° N., 2° W., heading for Denmark Strait.

Führer Conferences on Naval Affairs 1941

The first portion of the undertaking, that is, the break-through into the Atlantic, if possible unobserved, was regarded as the most difficult part of the operation. Previous experience had shown that enemy forces might appear in the Denmark Straits as well as in the Iceland-Faroes passage. Under suitable weather conditions it was considered certain that there would be enemy air reconnaissance in the Denmark Straits. The lightness of the nights made an unobserved break-through all the more difficult. On the other hand we could expect that air reconnaissance over the northern part of the North Sea would provide an adequate picture of the enemy's disposition, and that in the Denmark Straits, at the ice border, poor visibility would favour the break-through. Since so far it had not been established that British ships were equipped with radar, as a matter of fact, observations made so far seemed to indicate that they definitely were not so equipped, an unnoticed break-through was feasible.

Commander–in–Chief Leaves Scapa

The Commander-in-Chief in the *King George V* left Scapa at 2245/22; with him were the aircraft carrier *Victorious*, the cruisers *Galatea*, *Aurora*, *Kenya*, *Hermione* and seven destroyers. The *Victorious* had only just commissioned; she had been on the point of leaving for Gibraltar with a large consignment of crated Hurricanes and had only a small number of operational aircraft onboard. The battlecruiser *Repulse*, hastening up from the Clyde, joined the Commander-in-Chief off the Butt of Lewis in the forenoon of 23 May. All that day the fleet was steaming steadily to the westward. The weather was bad and the air patrols asked for could not be carried out. The Commander-in-Chief was some 230 miles northwest of the Butt of Lewis in about 60° 20' N., 12° 30' W., when at 2032/23 a signal came in from the *Norfolk*. The *Bismarck* had been sighted in Denmark Strait.

Führer Conferences on Naval Affairs 1941

If the visual reconnaissance in Scapa Flow in the afternoon correctly observed the actual situation, it must be presumed that the British forces, including the *Prince of Wales,* the *Hood,* and the *Victorious,* left Scapa Flow in the evening of 22 May and proceeded at high speed to take up waiting positions in the area southwest of Iceland.

On 23 May the Fleet Commander proceeded north of Iceland to break through via the Denmark Straits. The weather conditions were extremely favourable for his pupose; east wind, overcast, rain, moderate to poor visibility. At times visibility went down to 200 metres. Cruising speed of the group was 24 to 27 knots. The Fleet Commander considered the enemy disposition favourable. Air reconnaissance over Scapa Flow was impossible because of the weather. Again on 23 May the investigation of ice conditions in the Denmark Straits had to be abandoned.

Norfolk and *Suffolk* Find *Bismarck*

Between Greenland and Iceland there stretches a dreary expanse of Arctic waters frozen and icebound for a long distance from Greenland. On 23 May the ice edge on the Greenland side lay some 80 miles from the Iceland coast and between it and the minefields off the north-west of Iceland, the *Suffolk*, on the afternoon of 23 May, was patrolling on a south-westerly course at 18 knots. The weather conditions were unusual. The weather was clear over the ice pack and over the water for some ten miles from the edge of the ice. The rest of the Strait right across to Iceland was shrouded in dense mist. Evening was drawing on when at 1922/23 the *Suffolk* sighted the *Bismarck* and *Prinz Eugen* bearing 20° 7 miles (i.e., in 67° 6′ N., 24° 50′ W., or 55 miles N.W. of North Cape, Iceland). They were proceeding to the south-west skirting the edge of the ice. The *Suffolk*, sending out an "enemy report," made to the south-east to keep out of sight in the mist. The *Norfolk*, closing to make contact, sighted the enemy an hour later at 2030/23. They were only some six miles off and the *Bismarck* opened fire,[6] but the *Norfolk*, turning away, was not hit and sent out an "enemy report" signal at 2032/23. Though the *Suffolk* had been the first to sight the enemy, the *Norfolk*'s report reached the Admiralty first. It was received at 2103/23 and was broadcast. This was the first intimation received by the Commander-in-Chief, for the *Suffolk*'s signal had not reached him. It put the enemy some 600 miles away to the north-westward.

The battle fleet turned to 280° and increased to 27 knots. The *Hood* had received the *Suffolk*'s first report at 2004/23, which put the enemy about 300 miles 5° from the Battlecruiser Force. Vice-Admiral Holland turned to 295° and increased speed to 27 knots.

Dispositions

At the Admiralty, when the *Norfolk*'s signal came in, one of the first considerations was to safeguard the convoys at sea. Of these there were no less than eleven in the North Atlantic, six homeward and five outward bound. One of the most important was a Troop Convoy (WS8B) of five ships which had left the Clyde on 22 May for the Middle East escorted by the *Exeter*, *Cairo* and eight destroyers. As the *Repulse*, which was to have gone with it, had joined the Commander-in-Chief, Admiral Somerville's force at Gibraltar (Force H – *Renown*, *Ark Royal*, *Sheffield*) was called northward to protect it. The summons went out at 0050/24. Admiral Somerville's ships were clear of the harbour by 0200, carrying with them the *Bismarck*'s fate.

Führer Conferences on Naval Affairs 1941

At first there was nothing unusual to be observed in the enemy radio traffic, with the exception of an operational radiogram through blind transmission intercepted at 1254. This message, however, did not give any direct indication of enemy operations.

Norfolk and *Suffolk* Shadowing

All that night (23/24 May) the *Norfolk* and *Suffolk* hung on to the enemy, and all through the night their signals were going out. The enemy going 27 to 28 knots would be sighted, then lost in rain or falling snow; picked up with R.D/F, they would be seen looming dimly for a few moments through the gloom only to be lost again. But they were never wholly lost. "With great skill in very difficult conditions" (Commander-in-Chief report), the cruisers shadowed the enemy as they followed him to the south in a momentous and persistent chase. As the Arctic twilight gradually grew into day, the *Bismarck* could be seen some 12 miles to the southward. She appeared at 0325/24 to be turning to starboard and as the *Suffolk* turned to maintain her distance, the wind blowing half a gale from the north-west caught the aircraft on her catapult and disabled it. At 0445, a report was intercepted from the *Icarus*, one of the destroyers with the *Hood*, giving her position and that of the *Achates*, some distance astern of the *Norfolk*. This was the first intimation that Rear-Admiral Wake-Walker had of the Battlecruiser Force being in the vicinity. At 0516/24 smoke was observed on the port bow. The *Hood* and *Prince of Wales* were in sight.

Hood and *Prince of Wales*

When at 2054/23 the *Hood* shaped course at 27 knots to cut off the enemy, her six destroyers were told to follow at best speed if unable to keep up. They were able, however, to maintain their speed and were with her during the night. At 2318 they were ordered to form screen No. 4 ahead of the fleet. At midnight (23/24) reports put the enemy 120 miles 10° steering approximately 200°. The *Hood* was then steering 285° at 27 knots with the *Prince of Wales* 90° from her. The wind was north, blowing strong (force 4–5) with a moderate swell. Shortly afterwards (0008/24) speed was reduced to 25 knots and course was altered to north (0° at 0017/24). It was expected that contact with the enemy would be made at any time after 0140/24, and at 0015 final preparations were made and battle ensigns were hoisted. It was just then that the cruisers lost touch with the enemy in a snowstorm and for some time no reports were coming in. At 0031 the Vice-Admiral signalled to the *Prince of Wales* that "if enemy were not in sight by 0210 he would probably alter course to 180° until cruisers regained touch and that he intended both ships to engage *Bismarck*, leaving *Prinz Eugen* to *Norfolk* and *Suffolk*".[7]

The *Prince of Wales'* Walrus was ready for catapulting and it was intended to fly it off, but visibility deteriorated and it was defuelled and stowed away. It was then about 0140 and at 0147 the Vice-Admiral signalled "If battlecruisers turn 200° at 0205, destroyers continue to search to northward." Visibility was poor at the time and it is uncertain whether this signal was received by all of them. Course was altered at 0203/24 to 200°. As there was little chance by then of engaging before daylight the personnel was allowed to rest. At 0247 the *Suffolk* regained touch and by 0300 bearings were coming in again. The *Hood* increased speed to 28 knots at 0353, and at 0400/24 the enemy was estimated to be 20 miles to the north-west. By 0430 visibility had increased to about 12 miles and orders were accordingly given at 0440 to refuel the *Prince of Wales'* aircraft, but owing to delays, due to water in the fuel, it was not ready before the action commenced and being damaged by splinters and constituting a danger was jettisoned into the sea. The *Hood* was steaming hard at 28 knots to the south-west, on a course 240°; at 0450 the *Prince of Wales* was made guide of the fleet and *Hood* took station on her port bow (230°) resuming guide of the fleet at 0505. At 0510 first degree of readiness was ordered. Day was dawning out of the twilight. At 0535 a vessel could be seen looming on the horizon to the north-west. It was the *Bismarck*. She was some 17 miles away bearing 335°. The *Prinz Eugen* was ahead of her.

Führer Conferences on Naval Affairs 1941

What was most surprising, and of decisive importance for the further course of the operation, was the probability, established for the first time, that the enemy possessed evidently excellently functioning radar equipment. This eliminated entirely the advantage of poor visibility for the breakthrough of the task force, and prevented a swift escape from the enemy.

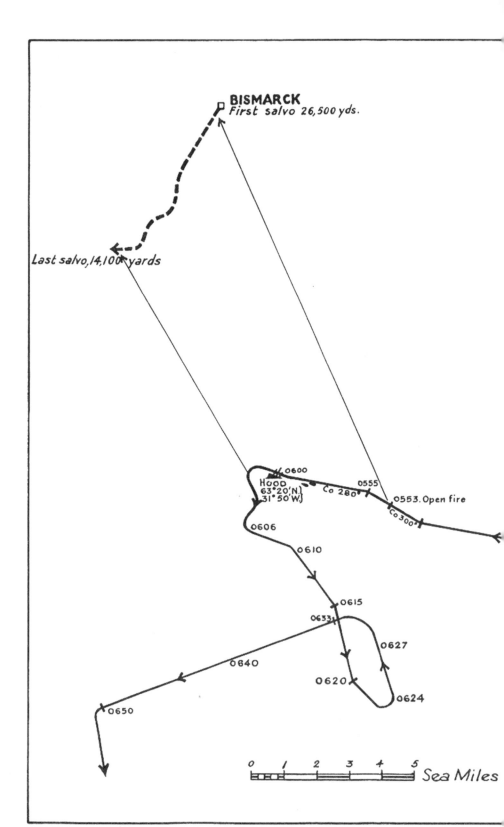

BISMARCK
First salvo 26,500 yds.

Last salvo, 14,100 yards

0600

HOOD
63°20'N.
31°50'W.

Co 280°

0555

0553. Open fire

Co 300°

0606

0610

0615

0633

0627

0640

0620

0624

0650

0 1 2 3 4 5
Sea Miles

C B. 3081. (3). 1942.

5017

H.M.S. HOOD AND PRINCE OF WALES
IN ACTION WITH
BISMARCK AND PRINZ EUGEN.
0553 TO 0613,
MAY 24TH 1941.

0530/24
PRINCE OF WALES
HOOD

Co. 240°, 28 knots.

0538 a/c 40° to starboard.

PRINCE OF WALES
HOOD.

Plan 2

(·From Prince of Wales' plan).

TSD/HS.(118)

Führer Conferences on Naval Affairs 1941

At 0543 on 24 May the battle cruiser *Hood* (Captain Kerr), flying the flag of Vice-Admiral Holland, and the battleship *Prince of Wales* (Captain Leach) made contact with the *Bismarck* and the *Prinz Eugen*. A running fight at a range of between 20,800 and 18,000 metres developed. Of the enemy ships, the *Hood* was ahead, the *Prince of Wales* astern. Both ships concentrated fire on the *Bismarck*. The *Bismarck* and the *Prinz Eugen* were proceeding in column. Both ships opened fire on the *Hood*, which was leading. She received several hits, and five minutes after the engagement began a hit on the stern, probably in the magazine aft, blew her up. Hydrophone observation enabled our ships to avoid several torpedoes from the *Hood*. After the destruction of the *Hood* both ships concentrated fire on the *Prince of Wales*. After certain hits from both ships had been observed she turned off amid clouds of black smoke and then was lost from sight for several hours. The *Bismarck* received two hits from the *Prince of Wales*, one of them a low shot beneath the side armour in section 13–14, the other in section 20–21. As a result the *Bismarck*'s speed was reduced; she went down by the bow 1° and the oil tanks were pierced, consequently leaving very strong traces of oil. The maximum speed of the *Bismarck* was 28 knots. In spite of several near hits, the *Prinz Eugen* did not suffer any damage.

65

Action with *Bismarck*

(Plan 2)

At 0537/24 the *Hood* and *Prince of Wales* were turned together, by blue pendant, 40° to starboard towards the enemy, and at 0541 the latter was stationed 080° from the *Hood*. At 0549, course was altered to 300° by another blue pendant turn. At 0549, the left-hand ship, the *Prinz Eugen*, was designated as the target by the signal G.S.B. 337 L1[8] but this was changed to the *Bismarck* by the signal G.O.B. 1[9] just before opening fire. By 0552½ the range was down to about 25,000 yards and the *Hood* opened fire. The *Bismarck*, which replied quickly and accurately, straddled with her second or third salvo. A fire broke out in the *Hood* near the port after 4-in. gun which quickly spread till the whole midship part seemed to be in flames, burning with a pink glow shrouded in dense smoke. The *Prince of Wales* opened fire at 0553/24, the first salvo being observed over and the sixth a straddle. It is not stated when the *Prinz Eugen* joined in, but she was firing practically throughout the action. The *Norfolk* and *Suffolk* were too far astern to take part in the action. The *Suffolk* indeed fired six salvoes at 0619 mistaking for the *Bismarck* an R.D/F range coming in from an aircraft. She was actually out of gun range from both the *Bismarck* and *Prinz Eugen* at the time. The cruisers do not appear to have been informed of the *Hood*'s position or her intention to attack.

At 0555 the two ships turned two points to port together by blue pendant. This opened the *Prince of Wales*' A arcs as she was firing her ninth salvo.

At 0600 *Hood* had a second signal "two blue" flying intending to turn another two points to port; the *Bismarck* had just fired her fifth salvo when the *Hood* was rent in two by a huge explosion rising apparently between the after funnel and mainmast. The fore part began to sink separately, bows up, whilst the after part remained shrouded in a pall of smoke. Three or four minutes later, the *Hood* had vanished beneath the waves leaving a vast cloud of smoke drifting away to leeward. She sank in 63° 20′ N., 31° 50′ W.

The *Prince of Wales* altered course to starboard to avoid the wreckage of the *Hood* and the *Bismarck*'s main and secondary armaments were quickly directed on her at about 18,000 yards. Within a very short time she was hit by four 15-in. and three smaller shells. At 0602 a large projectile wrecked the bridge, killing or wounding most of the personnel and about the same time the ship was holed under water aft. It was decided temporarily to discontinue the action and at 0613 the *Prince of Wales* turned away to 160° behind a smoke screen. The after turret continued firing but its shell ring jammed during the turn and the four guns of the turret are stated to have been out of action until 0825.[10] When the *Prince of Wales* ceased firing the range was 14,500. She had fired 18 salvoes from the main armament and five from the secondary. The *Bismarck*, which made no attempt to follow or continue the action, had not escaped unscathed. According to survivors' reports, she was hit three times. One projectile entering the port side forward, blew a hole in the starboard side under water and flooded three sections. Another struck the port side further aft below water, buckling some plates and flooding one section. The third passed over the deck without exploding but carried away the bows of the pinnace. Some survivors said the *Hood* hit with her third salvo and some thought that hit number two was scored by the *Prince of Wales*.

Such was the end of the brief engagement in the morning of 24 May. The loss by one unlucky hit of the gallant *Hood* with Vice-Admiral Lancelot Holland, Captain Ralph Kerr and her fine ship's company was a grievous blow, but a great concentration of forces was gathering behind the Commander-in-Chief and Admiral Somerville was speeding towards him from the South.

Signals sent from *Bismarck* to Group West

0552/24	Am engaging two heavy units.
0632	Battlecruiser probably *Hood* sunk. Another battleship *King George* or *Renown* damaged and turned off. Two heavy cruisers maintaining contact.
0705	Have sunk a battleship in approximate position 63 10N, 32 00W.

Fleet Commander

Note: *Prince of Wales* was mistaken for *King George V* throughout.

The Chase

When the *Hood* blew up, the *Norfolk* was 15 miles to the northward coming up at 28 knots. By 0630 she was approaching the *Prince of Wales*, and Rear-Admiral Wake-Walker, signalling his intention to keep in touch, told her to follow at best speed. The *Hood's* destroyers away in the north-east were ordered to search for survivors, but found only three.[11] The *Prince of Wales* reported that she could go 27 knots and was told to open out to 10 miles on a bearing 110° so that the *Norfolk* could fall back on her if attacked. Far off the enemy cruiser *Prinz Eugen* could be seen working out to starboard of the *Bismarck* while the chase continued to the southward.

At 0757 the *Suffolk* reported that the *Bismarck* had reduced speed and appeared to be damaged and shortly afterwards a Sunderland flying boat from Iceland, sighted at 0810, reported that she was leaving behind her a broad track of oil. The Commander-in-Chief with the *King George V* was still a long way off (about 360 miles to the eastward) and Rear-Admiral Wake-Walker on the bridge of the *Norfolk* had to make an important decision: was he with the help of the *Prince of Wales* to renew the action or was he to make it his business to ensure that the enemy should be intercepted and brought to action by the Commander-in-Chief. A dominant consideration in the matter was the state of the *Prince of Wales*. Her bridge had been wrecked, she had 400 tons[12] of water in her stern compartments, two of her guns were unserviceable[13] and she could not go more than 27 knots.[14] She had only recently commissioned and barely a week had passed since Captain Leach had been able to report her ready for service. Her turrets were of a new and untried model, liable to "teething" troubles and evidently suffering from them, for at the end of the morning action her salvoes had been seen falling short and wide. In a nutshell, it was doubtful whether in her then state she was a match for the *Bismarck*. It was on these grounds that Rear-Admiral Wake-Walker decided that he would confine himself to shadowing and would not attempt to force on an action. The forenoon passed. Soon after eleven the visibility began to decrease and the enemy was finally lost to sight at noon in a mist of drizzling rain. The *Prince of Wales* had closed in and was ordered to keep astern. She was still clearing up the wreckage of her bridge.

Führer Conferences on Naval Affairs 1941

After the victorious engagement the Fleet Commander continued to proceed south. The position at 1400 was in quadrat AK 11, which is about 240 miles east of the southern tip of Greenland. The *Prince of Wales* made off for the time being and the cruisers *Norfolk* and *Suffolk* maintained contact, which was later resumed by the *Prince of Wales* also. At noon the Fleet Commander announced his intention of making for St. Nazaire and of releasing the *Prinz Eugen* to carry on warfare against merchant shipping. If no further engagement ensued, he planned to withdraw during the night.

In the evening Group West sent a radio message (Radiogram 1842) agreeing with the Fleet Commander's proposal to send away the *Prinz Eugen* to take part in the war against merchant shipping, and expressing the opinion that in case the Fleet Commander is able to elude the enemy, it would seem expedient for the *Bismarck* to wait for some time in a remote sea area.

Signals sent from *Bismarck* to Group North

0801/24   1) Electrical engine room No. 4 broken down.

2) Port boiler room No. 2 is making water, but can be held. Water in the forecastle.

3) Maximum speed 28 knots.

4) Two enemy Radar sets recognised.

5) Intentions: To put into St. Nazaire. No losses of personnel.

Fleet Commander

Signal sent from *Bismarck* to Naval War Staff and Group West

1348/24   1400 approximate position 60 20N, 36 20W. *King George* with cruiser is maintaining contact. Intention: If no engagement, intend to attempt to shake off enemy during night.

Fleet Commander

Measures

The loss of the *Hood* increased the tensity of the situation. To watch for any attempt of the enemy to break back, the *Manchester, Birmingham* and *Arethusa* had been ordered at 0120/24 to take up a patrol north of Langanaes (N.E. point of Iceland). They were told to proceed there with all despatch.

The *Rodney*, which with four destroyers was escorting the *Britannic* westward, was ordered at 1022/24 to steer west on a closing course and if the *Britannic* could not keep up was to leave her with one destroyer. She was then some 550 miles south-east of the *Bismarck*. At 1200/24 in 55° 15' N., 22° 25' W., she left the *Britannic* with the *Eskimo* and proceeded with the *Somali, Tartar* and *Mashona* westward on a closing course. Two other capital ships were in the Atlantic – the *Ramillies* and *Revenge*. The *Ramillies* was escorting convoy HX127 from Halifax and was some 900 miles south of the *Bismarck*. She was ordered at 1144/24 to place herself to westward of the enemy and leaving her convoy at 1212/24 in 46° 25' N., 35° 24' W., she shaped course to the north.

The *Revenge* was ordered to leave Halifax[15] and close the enemy. The *Edinburgh*, 18th Cruiser Squadron, patrolling in the Atlantic between 44° N. and 46° N. for German merchant shipping was ordered at 1250/24 to close and take on relief shadower. At 1430/24 she reported her position as 44° 17' N., 23° 56' W., proceeding 320° at 25 knots.

The Rear-Admiral 1st Cruiser Squadron was told to continue shadowing even if he ran short of fuel so as to bring the Commander-in-Chief into action.

These were the principal movements ordered during the forenoon of 24 May.

Bismarck Alters Course to 180°

In the low state of visibility, the *Norfolk* and *Suffolk* had to be constantly on the alert to guard against the enemy falling back and attacking them. About 1320/24, the *Bismarck* and *Prinz Eugen* altered course to the south and reduced speed. The *Norfolk* sighted them through the rain only 8 miles off, bearing 223°, and had to turn quickly away under cover of a smoke screen.

It was 1530 when the *Norfolk* received a signal made by the Commander-in-Chief at 0800 giving his position at 0800/24[16], from which it was estimated that the Commander-in-Chief would be within range of the enemy about 0100/25. This was in fact, however, much in advance of the actual movements of the Commander-in-Chief, though it was not till 0100/25 that the *Norfolk* received the Commander-in-Chief's later signal of 2156/24 stating that he hoped to engage about 0900/25.

In the co-ordination of these widespread movements aircraft played a continuous and important part. At 1535/24 a Catalina,[17] in sight from the *Norfolk*, was able to supply her with a useful report of the position, namely that the *Suffolk* was 26 miles away and the *Bismarck* was 15 miles ahead with the *Prinz Eugen* ahead of her.

At the Admiralty the position was being watched with tense expectancy, and at 1545/24 Rear-Admiral Wake-Walker was asked to state (1) the remaining percentage of the *Bismarck's* fighting efficiency; (2) what ammunition she had expended and (3) the reasons for her frequent alterations of course. He was also asked his intention as regards the *Prince of Wales'* re-engaging and was told to keep a good lookout for U-boats.

To these questions he gave the following replies: (1) uncertain, but high; (2) about 100 rounds; (3) unaccountable except as an effort to shake the cruisers off. In reply to the last question he stated that he considered that the *Prince of Wales* should not re-engage until other heavy ships were in contact, unless interception failed; he considered it doubtful whether she had the speed to force an action.[18] This reply made it clear that the *Bismarck's* fighting power had not been materially diminished.

The afternoon drew on towards evening. Still the *Bismarck* and *Prinz Eugen* held on to the south while the *Norfolk, Suffolk* and *Prince of Wales* were still keeping her in sight.

At 1711/24, in order to delay the enemy if possible, by attacking him from astern, the *Prince of Wales* was stationed ahead of the *Norfolk*. The enemy was not in sight from the *Norfolk* at the time, but the argus-eyed *Suffolk* gave his bearing as 16 miles 152° while she herself bore from the *Norfolk* 12 miles 256°. At 1809/24 she was herself in sight from the *Norfolk* and was ordered to close to 5 miles. The *Bismarck* had drawn closer; she was apparently trying to waylay the *Suffolk* in the mist and, as the latter was making to the eastward, the *Bismarck* at 1841/24 opened fire; her salvoes fell short, but one or two shots came near enough to start rivets in the side plating of the cruiser aft. The *Suffolk* replied with nine broadsides before turning away behind a smoke screen.

The *Norfolk* seeing the *Suffolk* attacked altered course towards the enemy and she and the *Prince of Wales* opened fire,[19] the latter firing 12 salvoes. The engagement was short and was over by 1856/24, but though no one was hit it was long enough for two of the *Prince of Wales'* guns to go out of action again with mechanical defects. The enemy made no attempt to continue the fire, and Rear-Admiral Wake-Walker informed the *Prince of Wales* that till the Commander- in-Chief arrived, he did not intend to get closely engaged. After this brief interruption the chase pursued once again the tenor of its way, and as the cruisers were by this time entering an area where U-boats were reported to be operating, they started to zigzag.

Signal sent from *Bismarck* to *Prinz Eugen*

1420/24   Intend to shake off enemy as follows:
During rain showers *Bismarck* will move off on westerly course; *Prinz Eugen* to maintain course and speed until she is forced to alter course or 3 hours after leaving *Bismarck*. Following this she is to oil from *Belchen* or *Lothringen* and afterwards to engage cruiser warfare independently.
Executive on code word 'Hood'.

Fleet Commander

Signal sent from *Bismarck* to U-boats

1442/24   West boats collect in approx. position 54 10N, 42 10W at dawn. Am approaching from north. Intend to draw heavy units shadowing *Bismarck* through this area.

Fleet Commander

Situation at 1800/24

From the Admiralty at 2025 24 May, there went out a signal summarising the situation at 1800/24. The position, course and speed of the enemy were given as 59° 10' N., 36° W., 180°, 24 knots with the *Norfolk*, *Suffolk* and *Prince of Wales* still in touch. The Commander-in-Chief's estimated position at 1800/24 was 58° N. 30° W. with the *King George V*, *Repulse* and *Victorious* and 2nd Cruiser Squadron.[20] The *London*[21] in 42° 50' N., 20° 10' W. had been ordered to leave her convoy, and close the enemy. The *Ramillies* in estimated position 45° 45' N., 35° 40' W. had been ordered to place herself westward of the enemy.

The *Manchester*, *Birmingham* and *Arethusa* were returning from their position north-east of Iceland to fuel.

The *Revenge* had left Halifax[22] and was joining HX128. The *Edinburgh*[23] in approximate position 45° 15' N., 25° 10' W., had been ordered to close and take over stand by shadower.

Altogether, without counting destroyers, some 19 ships (3 battleships, 2 battlecruisers, 12 cruisers, 2 aircraft carriers) were on the move.

Signal sent from *Bismarck* to Group West

2056/24 Impossible to shake off enemy owing to Radar. Proceeding directly to Brest owing to fuel situation.

Fleet Commander

Signal sent to *Bismarck*

1504/24 1) English unit K3G made tactical signal at 1223 from appr. position 62 00N, 32 00W.

2) A/c reports 0825: Sighted 12 merchant ships, 4 destroyers, 030°, 8 knots. Visibility 10 sea miles. Position 56 35N, 14 45W. Position is not exact.

Group West

Signal sent from *Bismarck* to Group West

1508/24 *Hood* annihilated within 5 minutes by gunfire this morning at 0600. *King George* turned off after being hit.

24 May, Evening

At 2031/24 the *Norfolk* received a signal sent by the Commander-in-Chief at 1455 saying that the *Victorious* might make an attack about 2200/24 and the Rear-Admiral now waited hopefully for the air attack which he expected about 2300. By that time the enemy had been lost to sight but fortunately about 2330/24 the *Norfolk* caught a glimpse of her 13 miles off. Ten minutes later at 2343/24 the aircraft were seen approaching. They circled round the *Prince of Wales* and *Norfolk* and the latter was able to direct them to the enemy. An hour later (0009/25) heavy anti-aircraft fire was seen and the *Bismarck* was just visible as the aircraft attacked.

Signals sent to *Bismarck*

1511/24   1) Air reconnaissance of Scapa has started.

2) English unit made following to Scapa at 1329: One enemy battleship, 1 enemy cruiser bearing 223°, 8 miles, course 180°. My position 61 17N, degrees of longitude were not deciphered, 24 minutes west.

1) *Renown*, *Ark Royal* and *Sheffield* left Gibraltar on unknown course during night to 24.5.

2) Chief of third battle squadron (Canada) intended to send *Royal Sovereign* to Norfolk on 10 May. Probably into dock.

Group West

Signals sent from *Bismarck* to Group West

1914/24   Short engagement with *King George* without result. Detached *Prinz Eugen* to oil. Enemy maintains contact.

0028/25   Attack by carrier borne aircraft. Torpedo hit starboard.

0037   Further attacks expected.

0153   Torpedo hit of no importance.

Fleet Commander

Signal sent to *Bismarck*

0241/25   West U-boats have been ordered to proceed to the eastward.

Group West

HMS *Victorious* and 2nd Cruiser Squadron Detached

On 23 May the Commander-in-Chief had to consider the possibility of the *Bismarck's* breaking back to Norway, but after the loss of the *Hood* this eventuality became less likely and the Commander-in-Chief proceeded on a more southerly course (260° at 0800 then 240° at 1050/24). There still remained, however, the risk of her escaping by superior speed, unless her speed could be reduced by a torpedo attack. The only ship available was the *Victorious*. She had only just commissioned, her crews were inexperienced and having been on the point of starting for Gibraltar with a large consignment of crated Hurricanes to be flown to Malta, she had only nine Swordfish (Squadron 825) and six Fulmars (Squadron 802) available for a striking force. In view, however, of the urgency of the situation, the Commander-in-Chief decided that he must call upon her to make an attack, a call which under difficult conditions she answered "with splendid gallantry and success". It was 1440/24 when the Commander-in-Chief ordered Rear-Admiral 2nd Cruiser Squadron in the *Galatea* to proceed with the *Victorious* and his cruisers, the *Aurora, Kenya* and *Hermione*, to a position within 100 miles of the *Bismarck*, there to launch a torpedo bombing attack and maintain contact as long as possible. Steaming 28 knots[24] they went off at 1509/24 to find the *Bismarck*. Her position was known through the excellent reports coming in from the *Norfolk* and *Suffolk* and a sun-sight had given the *Galatea* a good position (58° 53' N., 31° 44' W.) at 2000/24. As it was clear that she could not get within 100 miles of the *Bismarck* until 2300/24 on account of the latter's turn to the westward during the exchange of fire at 1850/24 (see page 70), the Rear-Admiral decided to fly the planes off at 2200/24 when 120 miles from their objective. The wind was blowing fresh from the north-west when at 2208/24 the *Victorious* turned to 330° and reduced to 15 knots to fly off nine Swordfish torpedo bombers of 825 Squadron. The weather was as bad as it could be. The flying deck presented a chilly prospect of dark foaming seas, rain and scudding cloud in a leaden sky. The heavily loaded planes gathered way very slowly. They were off at 2210/24 and disappeared into cloud and rain squalls.

T. B. ATTACK
ON
"BISMARCK"
BY
825 SQUADRON
OF
H.M.S. VICTORIOUS.

MIDNIGHT 24/25 MAY 1941.

POSITION [APPROX]:- 57° 00' N.
36° 00' W.

SKETCH COMPILED FROM AIRCRAFT CREWS' NARRATIVES
NOT TO SCALE.

(FROM PLAN IN H.M.S. VICTORIOUS' REPORT).

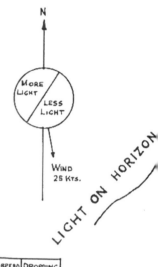

WIND
25 KTS.

LIGHT ON HORIZON

A/C LETTER	PILOT	EST TIME	EST RANGE	EST BEARING	EST HEIGHT	SIGHT SETTING	TORPEDO N°	DROPPING SPEEDS
A	LT. CDR ESMONDE	+30 S	1000ˣ	RED 45-60°	100-120'	24 KTS	508	110
B	LIEUT MACLEAN	ZERO	1000ˣ	RED 70°	100'	24 KTS	505	138
C	SUB-LT THOMPSON	+35 S	600ˣ	RED 60°	80-100	24 KTS	502	100
F	LIEUT GICK	+60 S	1200ˣ	RED 30°	40'	24 KTS REDUCED	62	95
G	LIEUT GARTHWAITE	+70 S	1000ˣ	RED 45°	50'	24 KTS	498	95
H	SUB-LT. JACKSON	+70 S	1000ˣ	RED 40°	50'	N.K.	517	N.K.
K	LIEUT POLLARD	+120 S	800ˣ	RED 30°	N.K.	N.K.	485	N.K.
L	SUB-LT LAWSON	+150 S	1000ˣ	GREEN 45°	80-100	24 KTS	478	120.
M	SUB-LT HOUSTON	–	–	–	–	–	509	–

TORPEDO SETTINGS
18" MARK XIIˣ
40 KNOTS.
31' DEPTH

PISTOLS
18" MARK II DUPLEX.
325ˣ SAFETY RANGE.

SEA & SWELL ... 31.
CLOUD ... 8/10ᵀᴴ AT 1200' [VARIABLE]
VISIBILITY ... 8 MILES [ON SURFACE].
SUNSET ... 0052 B/25
BAROMETER ... 997·5 mbs
TEMPERATURE. ... SEA 48°F
DRY 49°F.
WET 47·8 F.

NUMBER OF SQUADRON PRACTICE ATTACKS :- NIL.

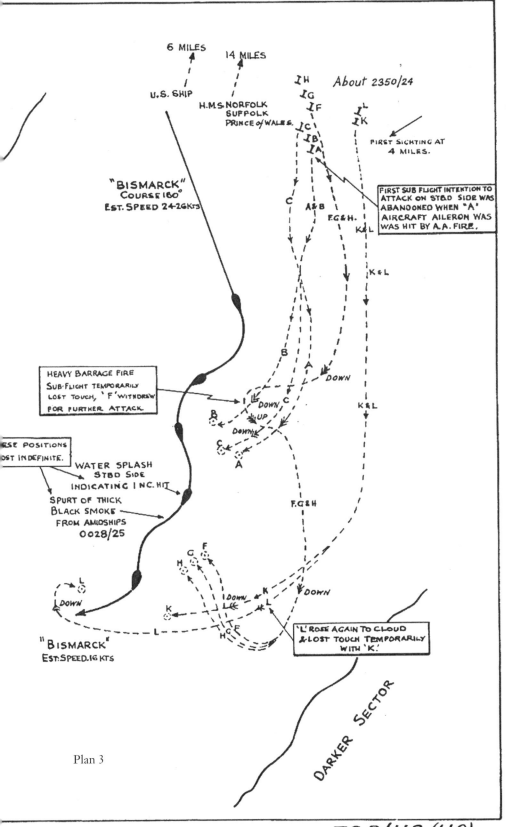

6 MILES

14 MILES

U.S. SHIP

H.M.S NORFOLK
SUFFOLK
PRINCE of WALES.

IH
IG
IF
IC
IB
IA

IL
IK

About 2350/24

FIRST SIGHTING AT
4 MILES.

"BISMARCK"
COURSE 180°
EST. SPEED 24-26 KTS

C

A & B

F.G & H.

K & L

K & L

B

A

DOWN

FIRST SUB FLIGHT INTENTION TO
ATTACK ON STBD SIDE WAS
ABANDONED WHEN "A"
AIRCRAFT AILERON WAS
WAS HIT BY A.A. FIRE.

HEAVY BARRAGE FIRE
SUB-FLIGHT TEMPORARILY
LOST TOUCH. 'F' WITHDREW
FOR FURTHER ATTACK.

DOWN C
B UP
DOWN
C
A

K & L

...SE POSITIONS
...OST INDEFINITE.

WATER SPLASH
STBD SIDE
INDICATING 1 NC. HIT

SPURT OF THICK
BLACK SMOKE
FROM AMIDSHIPS
0028/25

F.G & H

F
G
H

L
DOWN

K
L
DOWN K
L
DOWN

"BISMARCK"
EST. SPEED. 16 KTS

K
L
H G F

'L' ROSE AGAIN TO CLOUD
& LOST TOUCH TEMPORARILY
WITH 'K.'

DARKER SECTOR

Plan 3

HMS *Victorious,*
Aircraft Attack
(Plan 3)

The squadron led by Lieutenant-Commander (A) Eugene Esmonde took its departure from 58° 58' N., 33° 17' W. The *Bismarck* was estimated to be in 57° 9' N., 36° 44' W., steering 180°, 24 knots. The wind was 350°, 25 knots. The squadron went off on a course 225°, 85 knots, flying in broken stratus cloud at 1,500 ft. It was about 2327/24 when an A.S.V. instrument indicated the presence of a surface vessel 16 miles off on the port bow. Three minutes later through a gap in the clouds a glimpse was caught of the *Bismarck* steering 160°. Then the cloud thickened and she was lost to sight. As the striking force was estimated to be to the westward of the enemy, course was altered to north-east and then round to port. The instruments picked up two ships, one on the port and one on the starboard side. They turned out to be the *Prince of Wales*, *Suffolk* and *Norfolk* and the latter was able to direct them on to the enemy 14 miles on her starboard bow. At 2350/24 there were signs of a vessel ahead and below and the squadron broke cloud to deliver an attack. They found themselves over a United States Coastguard cutter lying stationary in the Atlantic swell. The *Bismarck* was six miles away to the southward and, sighting the aircraft, opened a heavy barrage fire. Lieutenant-Commander Esmonde pressed home his attack. It was close on midnight. The eight[25] planes that attacked were armed with 18-in. torpedoes, fitted with Duplex pistols set for 31 ft. At midnight, 24 May, three planes attacked simultaneously on the port beam. Three others made a longer approach low down attacking on the port bow a minute later. One took a longer course, attacking on the port quarter; one went round and attacked on the starboard bow a couple of minutes after midnight. At least one hit[26] was obtained on the starboard side abreast of the bridge. A Fulmar flown off at 2300/24 for shadowing saw a great column of dense black smoke rising from the *Bismarck* and reported her speed reduced. Two more Fulmars were flown off for shadowing at 0105, but in spite of "the utmost gallantry" were not successful in holding the enemy. Night was falling as the striking force returned (sunset at 0052/25); the homing beacon in the *Victorious* unfortunately failed; a rain squall hid the ship and the planes of the striking force missed her in the darkness. It became necessary to home them by R.D.F. and the beams of a signal projector. All were landed on by 0201/25. Two of the Fulmars which had left at 2300/24 were still missing and the homing beams kept circling round till 0250/25. It was dark by then and the Rear-Admiral 2nd Cruiser Squadron had regretfully to order the *Victorious* to extinguish them as their use in the vicinity of the enemy and of possible submarines was too hazardous. Both were lost, but the crews were saved after spending chilly hours in the Atlantic swell. Right up to 0258/25 long signals were coming from the *Bismarck* probably reporting the attack and possibly a recasting of Admiral Lütjen's plans. The *Prinz Eugen* may have parted company at this time. She was not seen after 1909/24.[27]

Führer Conferences on Naval Affairs 1941

Presumably the Fleet Commander thought that the chances of throwing off the enemy were much better in the south than in the north, and in particular his fear of enemy destroyers and planes, especially planes from the carrier *Victorious,* probably led him to rate the danger in the southern area as less than in the northern area.

Signals sent from *Bismarck* to Group West

0401/25   Enemy radar gear with a range of at least 35,000 metres interferes with operations in Atlantic to considerable extent. In Denmark Straits ships were located and enemy maintained contact. Not possible to shake off enemy despite most favourable weather conditions. Will be unable to oil unless succeed in shaking off enemy by superior speed. Running engagement at range of 20,800 metres to 18,000 metres. *Hood* concentrated fire on *Bismarck*. *Hood* destroyed through explosion after 5 minutes. After that target shifted to *King George* which turned off making black smoke after she received some hits and remained out of sight for several hours. Own expenditure of ammunition 93 rounds. After this *King George* continued action at maximum range. *Bismarck* received two hits from *King George* which reduced the speed and put oil bunkers out of action. *Prinz Eugen* succeeded in escaping because *Bismarck* engaged cruisers and battleship in fog. Own radar gear liable to break down, especially when own guns are firing.

Fleet Commander

Contact with
Bismarck Lost

While the aircraft of the *Victorious* were making their attack, the *Norfolk* sighted a ship to the south-west and gave the order to open fire. The *Prince of Wales* was able to identify it in time as an American coastguard cutter,[28] but in the movements preparatory to opening fire the *Norfolk* lost touch with the enemy for a time and it was not till 0116 that turning to 220° she suddenly sighted the *Bismarck* bearing 204° only 8 miles away. There followed a brief exchange of fire. The *Norfolk* and *Prince of Wales* turned to port to bring their guns to bear and the latter was ordered to engage. It was then 0130/25. The *Prince of Wales* fired two salvoes at 20,000 yards by R.D.F. and the *Bismarck* replied with two[29] which fell a long way short. The light was failing and the enemy was again lost to sight. By 0141/25 it was growing dark and in order to maintain contact, the *Suffolk*, which had the most reliable R.D.F. set, was told to act independently so as to keep in touch while the *Norfolk* with the *Prince of Wales* astern followed in close support. The chase continued while the *Suffolk* kept touch with the enemy who at 0229/25 was bearing 192° 20,900 yards and steering 160°. His speed had dropped to 20 knots. The night was light with a visibility of about six miles and the *Suffolk* resumed her zigzagging. At 0306 the enemy was located again. The bearing was the same. This was the last contact. The *Suffolk* at this time had commenced an outward zigzag of 30° which lasted ten minutes.[30]

When it was evident that the enemy was lost, the *Suffolk* signalled at 0401/25[31] to the *Norfolk* that the enemy had either worked round to eastward under their stern or turned westward and that he was acting on the latter assumption. At 0411/25 the *Suffolk* sent another signal stating that she had lost touch. This reached the *Norfolk* at 0504/25 and was followed by another made at 0505/25 and received at 0515/25: "Have lost touch with enemy at 0306". This signal made it clear that they had been out of touch with the *Bismarck* for over two hours. At 0552/25 the Rear-Admiral asked the Commander-in-Chief and the *Victorious* for an air search at dawn. The enemy had been lost. From examination of the plot it appeared to Rear-Admiral 1st Cruiser Squadron that the enemy must have made a large turn to starboard at about 0310. Accordingly at 0605/25, when it was growing light, the Rear-Admiral ordered the *Suffolk* to search to the westward and made a signal to the Commander-in-Chief: "Enemy lost at 0306B. *Suffolk* is being sent to search to westward. At daylight *Norfolk* follows *Suffolk* and *Prince of Wales* will be sent to join you." This signal, received in the *King George V* at 0607/25, upset the expectation of meeting the enemy at 0900/25. The enemy had slipped away in the treacherous twilight of a northern middle watch.

Signal sent to *Bismarck*

0846/25 Last enemy contact report 0213 from K3G. After that three figure tactical reports but no open position reports. We have impression that contact has been lost. Operational signals are repeated to Bermuda and Halifax but not to Gibraltar or Force H which is suspected to be in Eastern Atlantic.

Group West

Signal sent to Fleet Commander

1152/25 Heartiest congratulations on your birthday. May you continue to be equally successful in this coming year.

C.-in-C., Navy

Signal sent to *Bismarck*

1313/25 7 U-boats will form patrol line between appr. positions 47 10N, 15 10W and 45 00N, 10 50W. One U-boat in appr. position 47 50N, 16 50W.

Group West

Signal sent to Fleet Commander

1625/25 Best wishes on your birthday.

Adolf Hitler

Signal sent to *Bismarck*

1932/25 Strong air forces available for arrival *Bismarck*. Battle formations up to 14° west. Patrol line in accordance with my 1313 with 5 U-boats in appr. position 47 50N, 16 50W, and 47 50N, 12 20W.
3 destroyers for escort.
Outer channels of Brest and St. Nazaire under control. If necessary possible to put into La Pallice as well. Report when passing 10° west.

Group West

Search Measures

With the disappearance of the *Bismarck* at 0306 on 25 May the first phase of the pursuit ended. The Commander-in-Chief in the *King George V* with the *Repulse* in company was then about 115 miles to the south-east, bearing about 125° steering 210°. At 0616/25 Rear-Admiral Wake-Walker signalled that the probability appeared to be that the *Bismarck* and *Prinz Eugen* had made a 90° turn to the west or turned back and "cut away" to the eastward astern of the cruisers. The *Suffolk* was already searching to the south-west on a course 230° at 25 knots. The *Norfolk* was waiting for daylight. By 0630/25 the visibility was good and she proceeded to follow the *Suffolk* to the westward, at the same time detaching the *Prince of Wales* to the southward to join the Commander-in-Chief who was estimated to be then in 54° N., 34° 55' W.[32] Force H was instructed by the Admiralty to steer to intercept *Bismarck* at 24 knots. The instructions were received at 0330/25. Meanwhile the Rear-Admiral 2nd Cruiser Squadron in the *Galatea* had altered course at 0558/25 to 180° for the position where the enemy was last seen and the *Victorious* was preparing eight aircraft ready to fly off at 0730/25 for a search to the eastward. This plan, however, was altered on orders being received from the Commander-in-Chief to take the cruisers and *Victorious* and carry out a search to the north-west of the last reported position. (Commander-in-Chief 0600/25.) Five Fulmars had already been up during the night but had not been able to hold on to the enemy and two of them had not returned. The last one had flown off at 0400/25. It was 0716/25 when the *Victorious* got the Commander-in-Chief's order from Rear-Admiral 2nd Cruiser Squadron. Her Swordfish, the only planes available, were ranged ready. At 0800 she was in 56° 18' N., 36° 28' W. and seven of them flew off at 0810/25 to search between 280° and 40° for 100 miles. (Plans 4 and 5.) Their search was supplemented by the *Victorious* herself and the four cruisers of 2nd Cruiser Squadron (*Galatea, Aurora, Hermione* and *Kenya)* who steered to the north-west spread some miles apart (Plan 6). At 0919/25 the Admiralty sent out a report of the situation at 0600/25 giving the estimated position of the British forces at that time. Force H was estimated to be in 39° N., 18° 30' W., and was steering to intercept the enemy.[33]

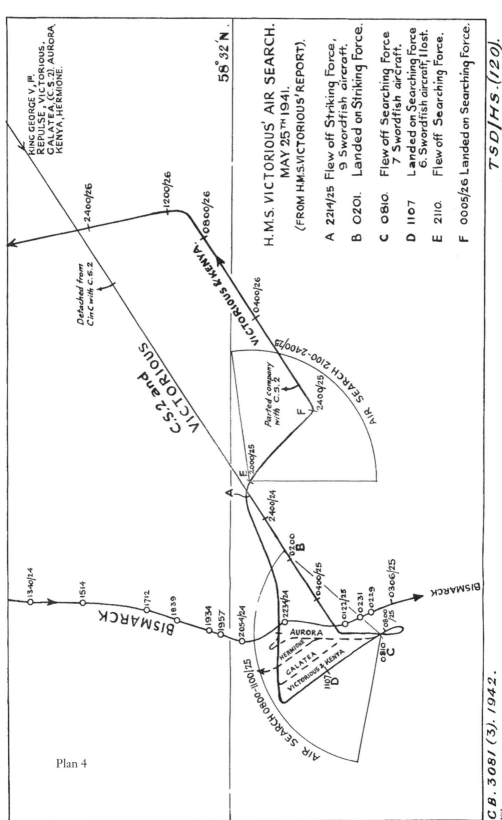

H.M.S. VICTORIOUS' AIR SEARCH.
MAY 25TH 1941.
(FROM H.M.S.VICTORIOUS' REPORT).

A 2214/25 Flew off Striking Force,
           9 Swordfish aircraft.
B 0201.   Landed on Striking Force.
C 0810.   Flew off Searching Force
           7 Swordfish aircraft.
D 1107   Landed on Searching Force
           6. Swordfish aircraft, 1 lost.
E 2110.   Flew off Searching Force.
F 0005/26 Landed on Searching Force.

58° 32′ N.

KING GEORGE V.,
REPULSE, VICTORIOUS,
GALATEA, (C.S.2). AURORA,
KENYA, HERMIONE.

Plan 4

T S D / H S . (120).

C B . 3081 (3). 1942.

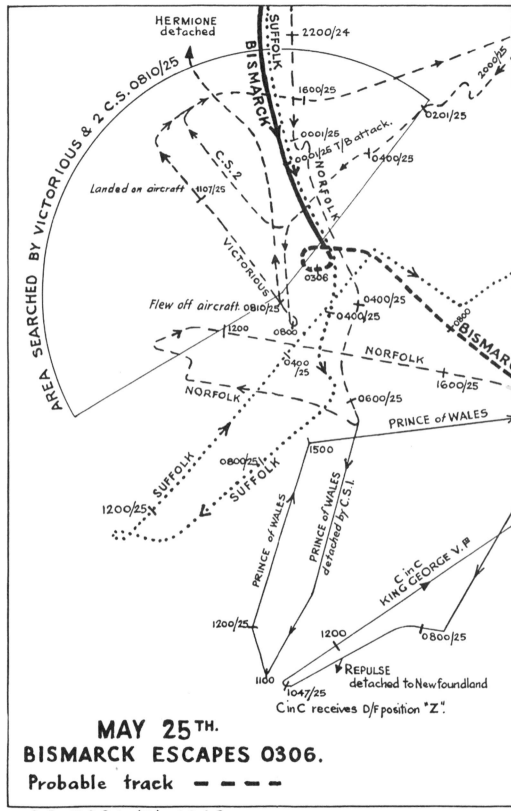

HERMIONE detached

SUFFOLK

BISMARCK

2200/24

1600/25

2000/25

0201/25

0001/25

0001/25 T/B attack.

0400/25

NORFOLK

AREA SEARCHED BY VICTORIOUS & 2 C.S. 0810/25

C.S.2

Landed on aircraft 1107/25

VICTORIOUS

0306

0400/25

0400/25

0800

BISMARCK

Flew off aircraft. 0810/25

0800

NORFOLK

1200

0400/25

1600/25

NORFOLK

0400/25

0600/25

PRINCE of WALES

SUFFOLK

0800/25

SUFFOLK

1500

1200/25

PRINCE of WALES

PRINCE of WALES detached by C.S.I.

C in C
KING GEORGE V.

1200/25

1200

0800/25

1100

1047/25

C in C receives D/F position "Z".

REPULSE
detached to Newfoundland

MAY 25TH.
BISMARCK ESCAPES 0306.
Probable track — — — —

C B. 3081. (3). 1942.

5017

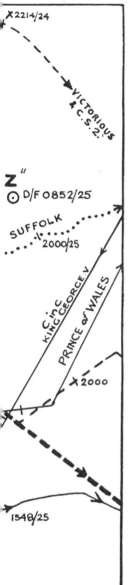

Plan 5

Führer Conferences on Naval Affairs 1941

25 May. Radio monitoring fixed the time of the last enemy contact report at 0213, the location, 56° 49' N. Enemy radio continued to be busy with urgent operational and tactical messages. Evidently at this time the enemy had temporarily lost contact. However, he regained it at dawn and according to the report of the Fleet Commander at 0700 on 25 May the *Prince of Wales* and the two cruisers were still shadowing the *Bismarck* in quadrat AK 55. From the radio traffic it can be gathered that the *Bismarck*, presumably making use of poorer visibility, succeeded in withdrawing from the enemy at about 1100 in the morning. As before, the enemy radio traffic was extremely busy. In the course of the day and in the evening and night several urgent operational messages from the British home area and the western part of the Channel were picked up, as well as messages communicating with Force H and with the 3rd Battleship Squadron (Canada), all pointing to comprehensive measures for searching for the *Bismarck*... At noon on 25 May the prevailing impression was that the enemy was concentrating his superior heavy forces for attack on the *Bismarck* in the sea area between 43° N and 52° N beyond the range of German aircraft, i.e., somewhat west of longitude 15° W. The enemy did not succeed in re-establishing contact in the course of 25 May. There could be no doubt about the gravity of the *Bismarck*'s situation at the time, however. There was no possibility of relieving her with our naval or air forces. In view of this situation, the Naval Staff suggested to the Fleet Commander to consider putting in at a harbour in northern Spain, should further developments make such action necessary. It is probably that the Fleet Commander, when he escaped from the enemy on 25 May, considered the possibility of withdrawing into the Atlantic. If he had done so for the purpose of refuelling from one of the tankers north of the Azores, the Fleet Commander might have succeeded in preventing the enemy from quickly regaining contact. Even a temporary withdrawal would have forced the enemy to stop his convoys or to resume protection of convoy routes by means of his fast forces as soon as possible. It must be assumed that owing to the fuel situation the Fleet Commander was unable to push out into the Atlantic in such a manner, and hence was forced to proceed directly to St. Nazaire, in spite of the great risk involved in such a course. Possibly the oil traces influenced his decision also.

T S D / H S (121).

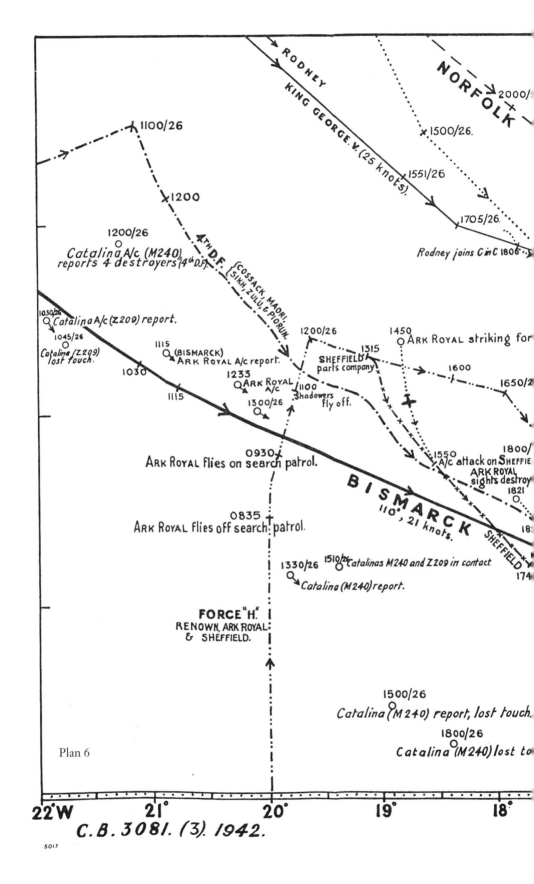

RODNEY

KING GEORGE V. (25 knots).

NORFOLK

2000/

1100/26

1200

1200/26
Catalina A/c (M240)
reports 4 destroyers (4ᵗʰ D.F.)

1500/26.

1551/26

1705/26.

Rodney joins C in C 1806

4ᵗʰ D.F.

COSSACK, MAORI,
SIKH, ZULU, & PIORUN.

1030/26
Catalina A/c (Z209) report.

1045/26
Catalina (Z209)
lost touch.

1030

1115

1115
(BISMARCK)
Ark Royal A/c report.

1233
Ark Royal
A/c

1300/26

1200/26

1450
Ark Royal striking for

1315
SHEFFIELD
parts company

1600

1650/2

1100
Shadowers
fly off.

0930
Ark Royal flies on search patrol.

0835
Ark Royal flies off search patrol.

BISMARCK
110°, 21 knots.

1550
A/c attack on SHEFFIE
ARK ROYAL
sights destroy

1821

SHEFFIELD

18

174

1330/26
Catalina (M240) report.

1510/26
Catalinas M240 and Z209 in contact.

FORCE "H."
RENOWN, ARK ROYAL
& SHEFFIELD.

1500/26
Catalina (M240) report, lost touch.

1800/26
Catalina (M240) lost to

Plan 6

22°W   21°   20°   19°   18°

C.B. 3081. (3). 1942.

5017

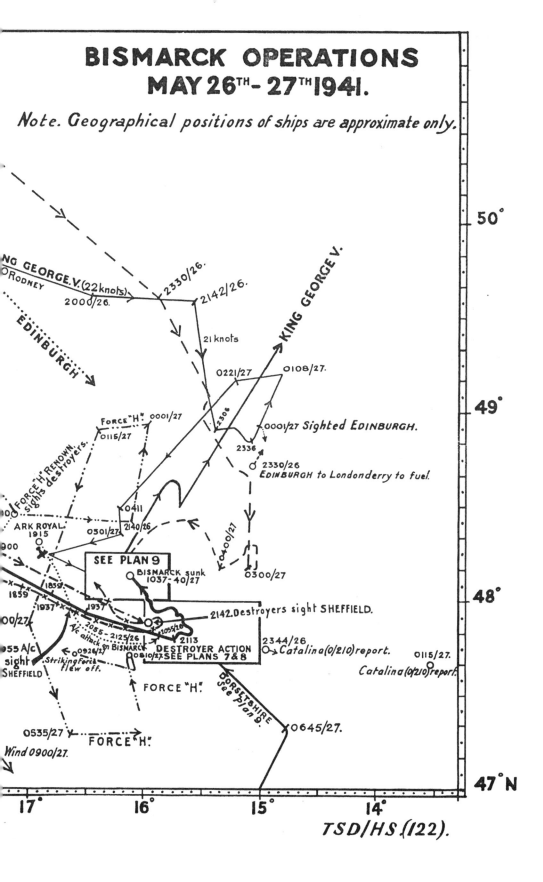

BISMARCK OPERATIONS
MAY 26TH- 27TH 1941.

Note. Geographical positions of ships are approximate only.

50°

NG GEORGE.V.(22knots)
O RODNEY
2000/26.

2330/26.

2142/26.

21 knots

KING GEORGE V.

EDINBURGH

0221/27

0108/27.

49°

FORCE "H" 0001/27
0115/27

2306

0001/27 Sighted EDINBURGH.

2336

2330/26
EDINBURGH to Londonderry to fuel.

FORCE "H" RENOWN. sights destroyers.

FORCE "H" RENOWN sights destroyers

0411

0501/27   2140/26

0400/27

0300/27

ARK ROYAL.
1915

900

SEE PLAN 9

BISMARCK sunk
1037-40/27

48°

x
1859
1859

1937 x

x
1937

2055 - 2125/26

2142. Destroyers sight SHEFFIELD.

00/27

2095/26

2113

2344/26
O→ Catalina(0/210)report.

0115/27.

955 A/c
sight
SHEFFIELD

A/c attack
BISMARCK

0092/27

Striking Force
flew off.

0810/27 SEE PLANS 7&8
DESTROYER ACTION

Catalina(0/210)report.

FORCE "H".

DORSETSHIRE
See plan 9.

0535/27 ···· FORCE "H".

Wind 0900/27.

0645/27.

47°N

17°   16°   15°   14°

TSD/HS.(122).

D.F. Position of 0852/25

The *King George V* was still proceeding to the south-west when at 1030 25 May "a series of D.F. bearings was received from the Admiralty which indicated that the enemy was breaking back across the Atlantic. The signals appeared to come from the same ship which had transmitted several signals soon after the T/B attack of the night before; they could therefore be reasonably attributed to the *Bismarck*. These bearings, as plotted in the *King George V*, showed a position too far to the northward which gave the misleading impression that the enemy was making for the North Sea."[34] This plot placed the enemy in 57° N., 33° W.[35] at 0852/25 (see Plan 6) and had an important bearing on the subsequent proceedings for "it gave the misleading impression that the enemy was making for the North Sea."

To counter this move the Commander-in-Chief turned round at 1047/25 to 55° at 27 knots to make for the Iceland-Faroes gap. The plotted position was broadcast and all Home Fleet forces were ordered to search accordingly. (Commander-in-Chief's signal 1047/25). The *Repulse* was no longer with him, having parted company at 0906/25 to proceed to Newfoundland to fuel. Meanwhile the *Suffolk* out to the westward had been covering all the enemy's possible courses to the south-west and, on receiving the Commander-in-Chief's signal (1047/25), turned to search to the eastward. Her search to the south-west had been fruitless. The search by the *Victorious* and *Galatea*'s cruisers to the north-west had been equally empty. Nothing had been sighted. The *Victorious* landed on her six Swordfish at 1107/25. One failed to return[36] and she remained for some time calling it. The *Galatea*, *Aurora* and *Kenya* on receiving the Commander-in-Chief's signal (1047/25) to search in the direction of the D.F. position had turned to 85°. The fuel state was beginning to affect them. The *Hermione* was down to 40 per cent, and had to be detached to Hvalifjord (Iceland). The remaining cruisers had to reduce to 20 knots to economise. The *King George V* still had 60.6 per cent left.

25 May

At 1100/25 the *King George V*, the *Suffolk* and the *Prince of Wales* were making north-eastward towards the D.F. indications of the enemy's position at 0852/25. The *Rodney* was in about 52° 34' N., 29° 23' W., some 280 miles to the south-eastward on the route to the Bay, and had decided at 0800/25 to remain there, but on receiving the Commander-in-Chief's signal (1047/25, see above) she too turned to 55° and proceeded eastward. Nothing had been seen of the enemy and his proceedings were shrouded in uncertainty. The Admiralty had, however, come to the conclusion that Admiral Lütjens was steering for Brest and at 1023/25 directions were sent to the Commander-in-Chief, Force H and 1st Cruiser Squadron to proceed on that assumption.[37] Rear-Admiral Wake-Walker, in the *Norfolk* had already come to this conclusion, and in view of the paucity of cruisers to the south-east was proceeding eastward on a course 100°. Meanwhile *Bismarck*'s course[38] seems to have been about 125° which would put her at 1100/25 about 165 miles east of the *King George V*, whose south-westerly track she seems to have crossed at 0800/25 about 100 miles astern. The heavy sea prohibited the use of the *King George V*'s Walrus, as it would have involved the loss of the plane and the exposure of the flagship to submarine attack while picking up the crew. "The accuracy of the information issued by the Admiralty throughout this stage of the operation and the speed with which it was passed out were beyond praise."[39] A clear view of the situation was given to all the forces concerned and the Commander-in-Chief was able to preserve wireless silence.

In the absence, however, of definite reports it was difficult to be certain of the position of the enemy. The D.F. bearings in the morning had not been very definite. At 1100/25 the *Renown* (Force H), then in 41° 30' N., 17° 10' W., was ordered to act on the assumption that the enemy was proceeding to Brest. She shaped course accordingly and prepared a comprehensive scheme of air search. At 1108/25, the *Rodney* was told to act on the assumption that the enemy was proceeding to the Bay. A couple of hours later a good D.F. fix at 1320/25 located an enemy unit within a 50-mile radius of 55° 15' N., 32° W. This was sent by the Admiralty to the Commander-in-Chief at 1419/25 (received at 1530/25). The enemy's route was still in doubt and at 1428/25, the *Rodney* was told by the Admiralty to cancel the signal of 1108/25 (giving the Bay as the enemy's destination), and to comply with the Commander-in-Chief's previous instructions,[40] on the assumption that the enemy was proceeding to Norway via the Iceland-Scotland passage. A couple of hours later, at 1621/25, came a query from Admiral Tovey who was still steering to the eastward, 80° at 25 knots – "Do you consider that enemy is making for Faroes?"

As evening drew on, opinion evidently hardened in favour of the Biscay destination, for at 1805/25 the Admiralty signal of 1428/25 to the *Rodney* was cancelled and she was told to act on the assumption that the destination of the enemy was a French port. Finally at 1924/25 the Commander-in-Chief and all other forces and vessels were informed that the Admiralty considered that the *Bismarck* was making for the West Coast of France. It was 1810/25 when the Commander-in-Chief turned accordingly to the south-east. He had no definite information. Aircraft had seen nothing. The *Victorious*, away to the northward in 57° 59' N., 32° 40' W. flew off six Swordfish[41] at 2110 to search between 80° and 180° for 100 miles. They saw nothing but the *Suffolk* (in 56° 55'N., 31° 17' W.). On the route to Biscay a sweep was flown by Coastal Command flying boats in the evening out to 30° W., but nothing was seen of the enemy, who probably crossed 30° W. at about 1600/25.

So ended, in an atmosphere of dimmed hope and dulled expectancy, a day of search and disappointment. The *Bismarck* was lost. Behind her lay the gallant *Hood*. In the south the *Renown* and *Ark Royal* breasting the heavy Atlantic seas were pursuing steadily their northward way.

Führer Conferences on Naval Affairs 1941

At 1030 on 26 May the *Bismarck* was sighted by a Catalina plane of Coastal Command, approximately in square BE 16, 600 miles west of Land's End. Anti-aircraft gunfire from the *Bismarck* caused the plane to lose contact...

26 May

By 26 May the question of fuel was becoming acute. For four days ships had been steaming hard on their momentous quest, and the Commander-in-Chief was faced with the stern reality of fuel limits. The *Repulse* had already left for Newfoundland; the *Prince of Wales* was on her way to Iceland; the *Victorious* and *Suffolk* had been forced to cut down their speed. Finally, about midnight, there went out from the Commander-in-Chief an ominous signal to say that he, too, might have to reduce speed to economise fuel.[42] At the Admiralty arrangements had been made for a comprehensive scheme of air search and in particular for two cross-over patrols[43] on the route to Brest by large Catalina flying boats fitted with long-range tanks. These were to start at 1000/26 from Loch Erne and were to have immediate and important results. Want of fuel was also affecting the destroyer screens. There was none available for the *Victorious*, but there were five of the 4th Flotilla,[44] escorting a troop convoy, WS8B, to the westward, and these were ordered at 0159/26 to join the Commander-in-Chief and *Rodney*. Leaving the convoy they shaped course to the north-eastward. They were to play an important part in the final stages of the chase. So, too, was Force H which was then nearing the immediate area of operations.

Signal sent to *Bismarck*

2344/25   Assume you will continue directly to French west coast harbour even if no contact with enemy.

1025/26   1) Reconnaissance started according to plan.

2) Weather situation in Biscay makes extended escort impossible. Therefore only close air cover possible for time being.

Group West

Force H, 26 May

The *Renown* was with the *Ark Royal* and *Sheffield*. They had had a rough passage against a heavy sea, high wind, rain and mist. The three screening destroyers had put back to Gibraltar at 0900/25. Two hours later, at 1100/25, in about 41° 30' N., 17° 10' W. (about 300' W. of Oporto) came a signal from the Admiralty to act on the assumption that the *Bismarck* was making for Brest. Course was altered accordingly to 360° and preparations made for a comprehensive air search. That evening the wind and sea increased and speed had to be reduced to 17 knots. At dawn on 26 May it was blowing half a gale from the north-west. They were in the latitude of Brest, and as no information of the *Scharnhorst* and *Gneisenau* had been received since 23 May, a security patrol was flown off by *Ark Royal* at 0716/26 in 48° 26' N., 19° 13' W. to search to the north and west.[45] At 0835/26 there followed an A/S patrol of ten Swordfish. With the ship plunging against a north-westerly gale the rounddown was rising and falling through a height as high as a house[46] while the planes were sliding bodily across the spray-drenched deck. The planes took off, landing on again at 0930. They had seen nothing. An hour later came the turning point of the chase.

Führer Conferences on Naval Affairs 1941

British reports stated that carrier aircraft from the *Ark Royal,* sent to carry out a torpedo attack on the *Bismarck* in the afternoon, met with no success. Obviously, due to the prevailing weather conditions the planes did not get near the *Bismarck* but passed her.

Bismarck Sighted

(Plan 6)

It was at 1030/26 that one of the Catalinas of the Coastal Command (Group 15) (Flying Officer Dennis A. Briggs) sighted the *Bismarck*. The report[47] placed the enemy in 49° 30' N., 21° 55' W. It was received in the *King George V* at 1043 and in the *Renown* at 1038.[48] It placed the enemy well to westward of the *Renown* and a wave of hope surged up in every ship. It was confirmed within an hour by two Swordfish from *Ark Royal* which were part of a searching force which had been flown off some time previously. They reported the enemy[49] at 1115/26 in 49° 19' N., 20° 52' W., some 25 miles east of the position given by the Catalina. The latter emerging momentarily from the cloud had come under a heavy fire, had been badly holed and had lost touch at 1045/26.[50] By the Catalina's report, the *Bismarck* was some 690 miles 96° from Brest,[51] which meant that at 21 knots she should reach Brest by 2130/27. The Commander-in-Chief was some 130 miles north of her and the *King George V* was steering to close, but it was evident that the *Bismarck* had too great a lead to permit of her being overtaken unless her speed could be reduced. Nor was the question one merely of distance and speed. The *Bismarck* approaching a friendly coast could run her fuel tanks nearly dry and was sure of air protection, while the British ships would have a long journey back in the face of air and submarine attack. The *Renown* was ahead of her, but it was important that she should not engage the *Bismarck* unless the latter was already heavily engaged by the *King George V* and *Rodney*; a signal to this effect was sent to Vice-Admiral Somerville at 1052/26 (received 1145). It remained for him to keep in touch and all that day shadowers from the *Ark Royal* were up sending in reports[52] while Force H took up a position within 50 miles ready to launch a torpedo attack. The two Catalinas were also sending in reports and one of them sighted the destroyers of the 4th Flotilla at 1200/26. When the Catalina found the *Bismarck* at 1030/26 the *Cossack* and her four destroyers were steering eastward to join the Commander-in-Chief. They seem to have crossed about 30 miles astern of the enemy's track about 0800/26.[53] The Catalina's report reached the *Cossack* at 1054/26 and "knowing that the Commander-in-Chief would wish him to steer to intercept the enemy", Captain Vian altered course to the south-east. They were to form that night an important link between the Commander-in-Chief and the enemy.

Führer Conferences on Naval Affairs 1941

In the afternoon reconnaissance signals from the aircraft led the cruiser *Sheffield* to the *Bismarck*. At 1824 the Fleet Commander reported the *Sheffield*'s position in quadrat BE 5311, course 115°, speed 24 knots.

Signals sent from *Bismarck* to Group West

1154/26 Enemy aircraft shadowing. Land plane. Appr. position 48 40N, 20 00W.

Fleet Commander

Signal sent to *Bismarck*

1156/26 English aircraft reports to 15th reconnaissance group: 1030 – one battleship 150°, speed 20 knots. My appr. position 49 20N, 21 50W.

1553 Enemy aircraft reports to Plymouth: Have lost contact with the battleship.

1773 English aircraft regained contact at 1600.

Group West

HMS *Ark Royal*'s First Attack

In a heavy sea and bad weather the *Ark Royal* was ranging a striking force. At 1315/26 the *Sheffield* was detached to the southward with orders to close and shadow the enemy, who was then estimated to be 40 miles south-west of the *Renown*. The visual signal[54] ordering this movement was not repeated to *Ark Royal*, an omission which had serious consequences (F.O. Force H despatch paragraph 21) for the aircraft did not know that the *Sheffield* had parted company. The interrogation of observers had caused some doubt in the *Ark Royal* whether the ship reported was a battleship or cruiser. Torpedoes with Duplex pistols were therefore adjusted for 30 ft. The striking force of 14[55] Swordfish were off at 1450/26 and making south. Weather and cloud conditions were particularly bad and reliance was placed in an A.S.V. set which located a ship some 20 miles from the estimated position of the enemy, that had been given to the leader on taking off. At 1550 they attacked through the cloud and fired eleven torpedoes. Unfortunately the supposed enemy was the *Sheffield*. Fortunately she was not damaged. Two torpedoes exploded on hitting the water and three exploded harmlessly astern. In the *Sheffield* there was an immediate appreciation of the mistake; she increased at once to full speed and did not open fire. The *Bismarck* was some 15 miles to the southward.[56] The striking force returned and were all landed on by 1720/26. About half an hour later, at 1740/26, the *Sheffield* sighted the *Bismarck* (in about 48° 30' N., 17° 20' W.) and, reporting her position, took station ten miles astern and began to shadow her closely for four fateful hours. The first relief shadowers from the *Ark Royal* were up and reported definitely that the ship was the *Bismarck*.

HMS *Ark Royal*'s Second Attack

The first striking force on its way back sighted Captain Vian's destroyers 20 miles west of Force H. This was the first intimation of their presence in the vicinity. As soon as the aircraft of the first striking force returned they were refuelled and rearmed at top speed. In view of the failures with Duplex pistols, they were replaced by contact pistols and the torpedoes were set to run at 22 ft. The second striking force, consisting of fifteen Swordfish (four of 818 Squadron, four of 810 and seven of 820), took off at 1910/26 and formed up in two squadrons of three subflights each, in line astern. Reports coming in from the *Sheffield* placed the enemy at 167° 38 miles from the *Ark Royal*. The force was ordered to get in touch with the *Sheffield* who was told to use D/F to guide them.

A strong wind, force 6, was blowing from the north-west, cloud was 7–10, 2,000 ft. The *Sheffield* was sighted at 1955/26 and lost; she was found again at 2035 and directed them by visual signal on to the enemy bearing 110°, 12 miles. The force took departure for the target in subflights in line astern at 2040/26, track 110°. Then followed the attack which was to have such big results. On nearing the enemy a thick bank of cloud with base about 700 ft. was met and in climbing through it the force got split up. At 2047/26, No. 1 subflight of three planes diving through the cloud sighted the enemy four miles off to the south-east down wind. One aircraft of No. 3 subflight was with them. Approaching again just inside the cloud they made their final dive at 2053/26 on the port beam under a very intense and accurate fire, dropping four torpedoes of which one was seen to hit. No. 2 subflight (two planes) lost touch with No. 1 in the cloud, climbed to 9,000 ft., dived on a bearing obtained by A.S.V. and attacked on the starboard beam under intense and accurate fire, dropping two torpedoes with one probable hit. The third plane of No. 2 subflight, having lost touch in the cloud, returned to the *Sheffield* to get another range and bearing, then flying ahead of the enemy carried out a determined attack on his port bow under very heavy fire and obtained a hit on the port side amidships.

No. 4 subflight followed No. 3 subflight into the cloud and got iced up at 6,600 ft. It dived and found a clear patch at 2,000 ft. where it was joined by the second aircraft from No. 3 subflight. The *Bismarck* was sighted engaging No. 2 subflight to starboard. The four aircraft circled her stern and diving through a low piece of cloud attacked simultaneously from the port side, dropping four torpedoes which did not hit. They came under a very fierce fire and one aircraft (4 C) was hit about a hundred times, both pilot and air gunner being wounded.

The two aircraft of No. 5 subflight lost contact with the other subflights and with each other in the cloud. They climbed to 7,000 ft. when ice began to form. Aircraft 4 K coming out at 1,000 ft. sighted the enemy down wind, went back into the cloud under fire, saw a torpedo hit on the enemy's starboard side, reached a position on the starboard bow, withdrew to five miles, came in just above the sea and just outside 1,000 yards fired a torpedo which did not hit. The second plane lost his leader diving through the cloud, found himself on the starboard quarter and after two attempts to attack under heavy fire was forced to jettison his torpedo.

Of the two planes of No. 6 subflight one attacked on the starboard beam and dropped his torpedo at 2,000 yards without success; the second lost the enemy, returned to the *Sheffield* for a new range and bearing and after searching at sea level attacked on the starboard beam but was driven off by an intense fire. The attack was over by 2125/26. Thirteen torpedoes had been fired and it was thought that two hits had been obtained; two torpedoes had been jettisoned.[57] The severe nature and full effect of the damage done was perhaps at first not fully appreciated. Actually the *Bismarck* had received a deadly blow. The last shadowers,[58] returning at 2325/26, had seen her make two complete circles. She had received two hits and possibly a third. One torpedo struck her on the port side amidships doing little damage. One struck her on the starboard quarter damaging her propellors, wrecking her steering gear and jamming her rudders. This was the one that sealed her fate.

The *Sheffield* was still shadowing astern when at 2140/26 the *Bismarck*, turning to port, opened fire with six accurate salvoes of 15-in.; none actually hit, but a near miss killed three men and seriously injured two. The *Sheffield* turning away sighted at 2142/26 the *Cossack* and her destroyers approaching from the westward and gave them the approximate position of the *Bismarck*. She had shadowed her closely since 1740/26 and had been able to direct the aircraft and destroyers on to her. Losing touch about 2155/26 she continued on what she thought was a parallel course to the northward. The destroyers went on to shadow and attack. In the *Ark Royal* aircraft were being got ready for an attack at dawn. Meanwhile the *Renown* and *Ark Royal* shaped course to the southward so as to leave the road clear for the Commander-in-Chief.

Signals sent from *Bismarck* to Group West

1903/26 Fuel situation urgent. When can I expect fuel?

2054/26 Am being attacked by carrier borne aircraft.

2015/26 Ship no longer manoeuvrable.

2105/26 Appr. position 47 40N, 14 50W. Torpedo hit aft.

2115/26 Torpedo hit amidships.

Fleet Commander

Signals sent to *Bismarck*

2117/26 U-boat reports: 2000. One battleship, one aircraft carrier in appr. position 47 50N 16 50W. Course 115°, high speed.

2205/26 U-boats ordered to collect in appr. position 47 40N, 14 50W.

Group West

Signals sent from *Bismarck* to Group West

2325/26 Am surrounded by *Renown* and light forces.

2140/26 Ship no longer manoeuverable. We fight to the last shell. Long live the Führer.

2358/26 To the Führer of the German Reich Adolf Hitler. We fight to the last in our belief in you my Führer and in the firm faith in Germany's victory.

2359/26 Armament and engines still intact. Ship however cannot be steered with engines.

Fleet Commander

The *Bismarck*, 26 May

The *Bismarck* could no longer steer. The steering motor room was flooded up to the main deck and the rudders were jammed. Divers went down to the steering room and managed to centre one rudder, but the other remained irreparably jammed.

The crew had been full of elation at the destruction of the *Hood* but by 25 May it became known that strong forces were pursuing them. Survivors stated that half a day was lost by unreliable reports from German planes.[59] Her course was being directed by Admiral Carls (Commander-in-Chief Western Group), and she was expecting to be met by a strong force of aircraft and submarines. She was urgently in need of fuel. When the torpedo hit her,[60] frantic efforts were made to repair the damage. About 2242 the British destroyers were sighted and a heavy fire opened on them. Their appearance must have greatly complicated the situation. About 2250/26 came a signal from Hitler: "All our thoughts are with our victorious comrades".

Captain Vian's Flotilla Makes Contact

Just as the sun was setting[61] Captain Vian (D.4) in the *Cossack* with the *Maori*, *Zulu*, *Sikh* and the Polish destroyer *Piorun* arrived most opportunely on the scene.

Shortly after 1900/26 Force H and the *Ark Royal*, who was just about to fly off her striking force to attack the *Bismarck*, had been sighted to the northward. Continuing to the south-eastward, the destroyers sighted the *Sheffield* at 2152, and obtained from her the approximate position of the enemy. As the last light was dying, the *Cossack* and her destroyers came creeping swiftly up.

They were spread 2.5 miles apart on a line of bearing 250°–070° in the order from N.E. to S.W. *Piorun*, *Maori*, *Cossack*, *Sikh*, *Zulu*: during the latter stages of the approach, speed was reduced and the flotilla manoeuvred so as to avoid making a high speed end-on contact.

At 2238 the *Piorun* on the port wing reported the *Bismarck* 9 miles distant, bearing 145° and steering to the south-eastward.

Destroyer Shadowing Operations

At the time of the *Piorun*'s report, the destroyers were steering 120°. They were at once ordered to take up shadowing positions, and four minutes later the *Bismarck* opened a heavy fire with main and secondary armaments on the *Piorun* and *Maori*. Two attempts were made by these ships to work round to the northward of the enemy, but they were silhouetted against the north-western horizon, and the *Bismarck*'s fire was unpleasantly accurate, though neither ship was actually hit. The captain of the *Maori* therefore decided to work round to the southward, and altered course accordingly.

The *Piorun* closed the range, and herself opened fire at 13,500 yards but after firing three salvoes, she was straddled by a salvo which fell about 20 yards from the ship's side, and, ceasing fire, she turned away to port under smoke. During this engagement, she lost touch with the British destroyers, and her movements thereafter are somewhat uncertain. She remained under fire for about an hour, fortunately without suffering damage, and during this time appears to have worked round to the north and east of the *Bismarck*, with whom she eventually lost touch at 2355.

The remainder of the destroyers, meanwhile, had been working round to the southward of the enemy to take up shadowing positions to the eastward of him. Soon after the initial contact, it was evident that the *Bismarck*'s speed had been so seriously reduced that interception by the battlefleet was certain, provided she could be held. In these circumstances, Captain Vian defined his object as firstly, to deliver the enemy to the Commander-in-Chief at the time he desired; and secondly, to sink or immobilise her with torpedoes during the night, provided the attack should not involve the destroyers in heavy losses. Accordingly, a signal was made at 2248/26 ordering them to shadow, and this operation was continued throughout the night, though torpedo attacks were carried out later under cover of darkness.

As darkness came on, the weather deteriorated and heavy rain squalls became frequent. Visibility varied between 2½ miles and half a mile but the *Bismarck*, presumably using R.D.F., frequently opened accurate fire outside these ranges.

About half an hour after sunset, the destroyers were ordered at 2324 to take up stations preparatory to carrying out a synchronised torpedo attack. This was subsequently cancelled on account of the adverse weather conditions, and they were ordered to attack independently as opportunity offered.[62]

At about 2300 the *Bismarck* had altered course to the north-westward: this general direction, apart from periodical drastic alterations to open her A arcs, or to avoid torpedoes, or to throw off the shadowing destroyers, she maintained for the rest of the night.

At this time the *Zulu* was in touch with her, and kept her under observation from the southward. At 2342 the enemy opened fire on the *Cossack*, then about 4 miles to the S.S.W., and shot away her aerials. The *Cossack* turned away under cover of smoke, shortly afterwards resuming her course to the eastwards, and gradually hauling to the northward.

A few minutes later, at 2350, the *Zulu* came under heavy fire from the *Bismarck's* 15-in. guns: the first three salvoes straddled, wounding an officer and 2 ratings. Drastic avoiding action was taken, as a result of which the *Zulu* lost touch. The *Sikh*, however, who had lost sight of the enemy half an hour previously, had observed her firing at the *Cossack*, and now succeeded in shadowing from astern until 0020, when the battleship made a large alteration to port and opened fire on her. The *Sikh* also altered course to port, intending to fire torpedoes, but the view of the Torpedo Control Officer was obscured by shell splashes, and she withdrew to the southward without making an attack.

During this engagement, the *Maori* was close on the *Sikh's* beam;[63] she now took up the shadowing, and at 0025 reported the *Bismarck's* course as 230°, but lost touch a few minutes later, probably on account of the enemy altering back to the north-westward.

For the next half hour, it seems that no destroyer was in touch with the *Bismarck*. Star shell were fired by the *Maori* at 0052 to indicate the position in which she had last been seen: but nothing was sighted until she was picked up again by the *Zulu* at 0100.

Destroyer Night Torpedo[64] Attacks

The *Zulu*, after her escape at 2345/26, had steered to the northward, and at about 0030 fell in with the *Cossack*. Shortly afterwards she sighted the *Piorun*. On receipt of a signal from Captain D.4, timed 0040, to take any opportunity to fire torpedoes, the *Zulu* altered to the westward, and at 0100 sighted the *Bismarck* steering 340°.

The position at this time was roughly as follows: To the northeastward of the enemy,[65] the *Cossack* was working round to the north and west. The *Maori*, since losing touch, had been making to the westward, and was now to the southwest of the quarry. The *Sikh*, having received no information as to the *Bismarck*'s course since the *Maori*'s report at 0025, had assumed her to be steering 230°, and was some distance to the southward.

At the time of sighting (0100/27) the *Zulu* was right astern of the enemy. Commander Graham states that his former experience that night had warned him to refrain from using W/T, and to keep altering his bearing. He therefore ran up on her port quarter, zigzagging at 25 knots. She did not appear to have seen the *Zulu*, who turned in towards her when she bore 090°, the range being estimated as 5,000 yards. The *Bismarck*, who at some time during this approach had altered course to 040°, at once opened fire with her main and secondary armaments and straddled the *Zulu*. Four torpedoes were fired at 0121: no hit was observed, and they are believed to have missed ahead. Commander Graham then ran well out to the northward, in order to be clear of other destroyers, and shortly afterwards witnessed a successful attack by the *Maori*.

The latter ship had seen the *Bismarck* open fire on the *Zulu* at 0107: three minutes later she reported the course of the enemy as 040°, and then closed slowly on the port quarter to 4,000 yards apparently undetected. When abeam of the enemy, who then appeared to be altering course to starboard, Commander Armstrong fired a star shell the better to see what he was about. Two minutes later, at 0137, two torpedoes were fired, and course was altered towards the *Bismarck*, with the intention of attacking again from her starboard bow when she should have steadied on her new course. Whilst the *Maori* was turning, a hit was observed on the enemy. A bright glow illuminated the water line of the ship from end to end, and shortly afterwards there appeared between the bridge and the stem a very vivid glare, which may have been a second hit. A cheer went up from the men at their action stations, exhilarating to all on the bridge and down below. The enemy immediately opened a very heavy fire with both main and secondary armaments and quick-firing guns. As the *Maori* was being straddled, she turned away, and increased to full speed; shots continued to fall on both sides of the ship until the range had been opened to 10,000 yards, but she was not actually hit. To quote her Captain's report, "it was quite an exciting few minutes". It must have been equally exciting for the *Bismarck*, for Captain Vian in the *Cossack* had meanwhile been creeping up from the north-eastward and at 0140, only three minutes after the *Maori's* attack, fired three torpedoes from a range of 6,000 yards.

The battleship stood out plainly, silhouetted by the broadsides she was firing at the *Maori*, and one unmistakable hit was obtained. Flames blazed up on her forecastle visible to all ships after these attacks, though they were quickly extinguished. Probably in consequence of these hits, the enemy now stopped, a fact which was reported by the *Zulu* at 0148, and did not get under way again until about an hour later. On receipt of this report, Commander Stokes in the *Sikh* who was closing the scene of action from the southward, decided to carry out a deliberate unseen attack. Accordingly, after verifying by R.D.F. that the *Bismarck* was indeed stopped, he fired four torpedoes at 0218 at 7,000 yards, which from previous experience that night he judged to be the shortest range from which an attack could be launched undetected. One hit was believed to have been obtained.[66] After this attack, the *Sikh* remained in R.D.F. contact with the enemy until 0359, when she lost touch.

At about 0240, the *Bismarck* seems to have got under way again, proceeding very slowly to the north-westward. At 0335 another attack on her was made by the *Cossack*, who fired one torpedo from a position 4,000 yards to the north of her. No hit was claimed and the *Cossack* coming under a heavy fire, which was seen by the other destroyers, withdrew to the northward under cover of smoke, altering to a westerly course shortly afterwards.

At 0400 all touch with the enemy was lost for a time. The *Cossack* was then to the west-north-westward of the *Bismarck*, and the *Sikh*, *Zulu* and

Maori were between south-west and south-east of her. All the destroyers now endeavoured to regain contact, the *Cossack* working to the west and south-west, and the remaining three to the north-westward while doing so, in order to get the enemy between them and the eastern horizon before dawn.[67]

At 0435 the *Zulu* was illuminated by star-shell, probably fired by one of her consorts: she turned away to the westward but the *Bismarck* did not open fire.

Touch does not seem to have been regained until shortly before 0600, but Captain Vian was quite confident that the enemy would not be able to elude him, and at 0500 ordered the *Piorun*, who was short of fuel, to proceed to Plymouth.[68] The *Piorun* had by this time apparently worked round to the south-eastward of the *Bismarck*, and was then searching in a north-westerly direction. This Commander Plawski continued to do till 0600, before shaping course for harbour.

Destroyers Shadowing and Final Torpedo Attack

Touch was regained by the *Maori*, who at 0550/27 sighted the *Bismarck* zigzagging slowly either side of 340° at about 7 knots and thereafter shadowed her till daylight. At 0625 a star-shell fired by her shone out close to the starboard beam of the *Sikh*, who immediately afterwards sighted the *Bismarck* emerging from a rain squall, 7,000 yards on her starboard bow. It was then nearly full daylight, but greatly to the surprise of Commander Stokes, the *Sikh* got away unfired at.

Shortly before sunrise, a final torpedo attack was carried out by the *Maori*, who fired two torpedoes at a range of 9,000 yards at 0656 which apparently did not hit. The *Bismarck* opened fire on her and straddled; she escaped undamaged at 28 knots.

OPERATIONS AGAINST BISMARCK
23~27th MAY 1941
4TH DESTROYER FLOTILLA
MOVEMENTS 2230/26th to 2400/26th

BISMARCK	———————
COSSACK	———————
MAORI	··············
ZULU	— · —— · —— ·
SIKH	— — — —

From Captain 4th D.F., report M 08780/41.

C B. 3081 (3). 1942.

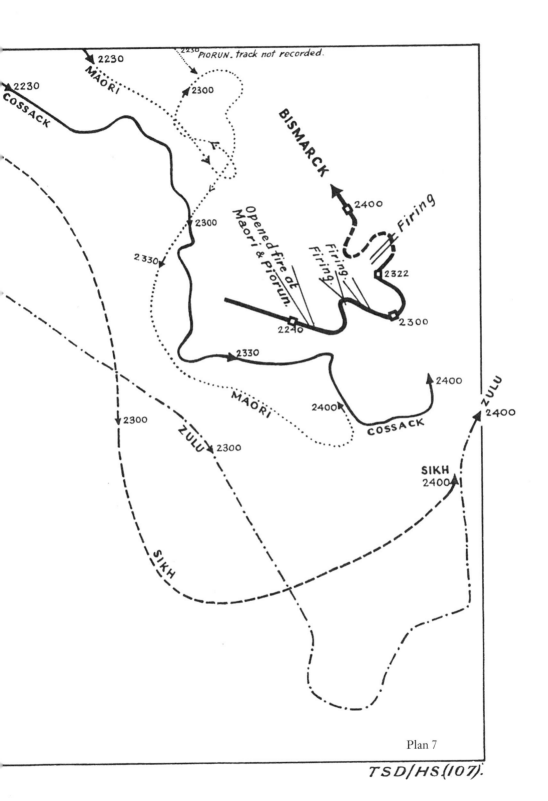

2230
MAORI
2230
COSSACK
2230 PIORUN. track not recorded.
2300
BISMARCK
2300
2330
2300
2400
Firing
Opened fire at Maori & Piorun.
Firing.
Firing.
2322
2240
2300
2330
MAORI
2400
2400
ZULU
2400
2300
ZULU 2300
COSSACK
SIKH
2400
SIKH
ZULU

Plan 7

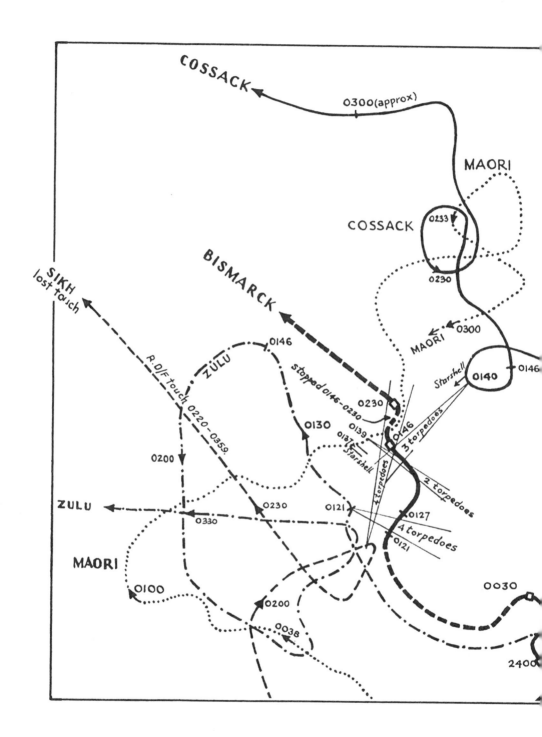

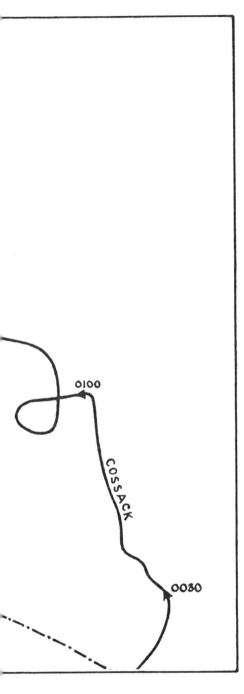

Plan 8

At daylight the destroyers were stationed in four sectors from which they were able to keep the enemy under continuous observation until the arrival of the Battle Fleet at 0845.

The conduct of the night operations had been "a model of its kind" (Commander-in-Chief's despatch, paragraph 76). In heavy weather, frequently under fire, they had hung on to their prey with the utmost determination, hit her with two torpedoes and brought her to the Commander-in-Chief without suffering damage to themselves. They now took up a position to watch the battle and to see the final destruction of an enemy which they had done so much to ensure.

The Eve of Battle

Force H

While the destroyers were shadowing the *Bismarck*, the pursuing forces were drawing steadily closer. To the north was the Commander-in-Chief with the *King George V* and *Rodney*, with the *Norfolk* closing on them. In the south the *Dorsetshire* was coming up, while Force H was waiting for the dawn. When Captain Vian's destroyers got in touch at 2251/26 the *Renown* and *Ark Royal* were north-west of the enemy. It was not possible to carry out a third attack that night, but all preparations were made for an attack with 12 planes at dawn. Course was shaped to the northward and then westward for a time (see Plan 6) and at 0115/27 Force H turned south. Shortly afterwards (at 0138/27) came instructions from the Commander-in-Chief to keep not less than 20 miles to southward of the *Bismarck* so as to leave a clear approach for the Battle Fleet. Force H accordingly continued to the southward during the night. Periodical bursts of starshell and gunfire could be seen to the eastward during the destroyer attacks. At 0509/27, a plane was flown off in the darkness to act as spotter for the *King George V*. It was blowing a gale and the plane lost its position in heavy rainclouds and did not find the enemy. The striking force of twelve planes were ready, but owing to low visibility the dawn[69] attack was cancelled. At 0810 the *Maori* was sighted to the northward; she reported the *Bismarck* 11 miles north of her. This made the enemy 17 miles from the *Renown* and course was shaped to the south-west. At 0915 heavy gunfire could be heard and the striking force was flown off. It found the *Bismarck* at 1016/27. The battle was over; her guns were silenced; she was on fire. They saw her sink. It was 1115/27 when they got back to the *Ark Royal*. A Heinkel hovering round dropped a couple of bombs near while they were landing on.

HMS *Norfolk*

When the Catalina report (1030/26) came in, the *Norfolk* altered course to the south-east and went on to 27 knots. At 2130/26, the *Bismarck* was still some 160 miles to the southward and speed was increased to 30 knots (Plan 6). At 2228/26 came the report of the hit by the *Ark Royal's* aircraft and the *Norfolk* turned to the southward, continuing to close the enemy, guided by the flashes of starshell from the destroyers, with the intention of keeping to the northward of him so as to be in a position to flank mark for the Commander-in-Chief. Day light. Nothing in sight at first, but steering down the destroyers' last D.F. bearing the *Bismarck* was sighted to the southeast at 0753/27, bearing 145° 9 miles. She did not open fire and was lost to sight in ten minutes. Quarter of an hour later (at 0821/27) the Commander-in-Chief was sighted to the westward, 12 miles away, and the bearing and distance of the enemy (130° 16 miles) were passed to him. The action opened at 0847/27. The *Norfolk* was then some 10 miles from the Commander-in-Chief and almost due north of the *Bismarck*. She had seen the beginning and was to see the end.

HMS *Dorsetshire*

The *Dorsetshire* on 26 May was bringing home a Sierra Leone convoy. When the Catalina's report of the enemy came in at 1056/26, she was some 360 miles south of the *Bismarck*. Leaving the armed merchant cruiser *Bulolo* to look after the convoy she shaped course to the northward to take up the possible task of shadowing. By 2343/26 it was clear from reports that the *Bismarck* was making no ground to the eastward and at 0230/27 she appeared to be lying stopped. A very heavy sea was running and the *Dorsetshire* plunging into it was forced to reduce speed to 25 and later to 20 knots. At 0833/27 a destroyer was sighted ahead bearing 294° 8 miles. She was challenged. It was the *Cossack* who reported the enemy 290° 6 miles. At 0850/27, the flashes of the *Bismarck's* guns could be seen to the westward. The *Dorsetshire* had reached the scene of action in the nick of time having steamed 600 miles since the enemy report came in.

The Commander-in-Chief and *Rodney*

All through 26 May, the Commander-in-Chief, in the *King George V*, had been making hard to the south-east at 25 knots. He had been joined by the *Rodney* at 1806/26. They were then some 90 miles north of the *Bismarck*. Fuel was a matter of grave anxiety. At noon, 26 May, the *King George V* had only 32 per cent remaining and the *Rodney* reported that she would have to turn back at 0800/27. Speed had to be reduced on this account to 22 knots at 1705/26. In these circumstances it was no longer possible to hope to intercept the enemy, and the Commander-in-Chief decided that unless the enemy's speed had been reduced by 2400/26, he must turn at that hour. The only hope lay in the *Bismarck* being slowed up by torpedo bombers. The prospects were not too favourable and the faces of those examining the charts reflected the gloom of the sky. The evening drew on. A report came in of the *Ark Royal's* striking force having left. Then at 2136/26 came in a report from the *Sheffield* that the enemy was steering 340°; four minutes later came another, giving her course as 0°. These reports indicated that she was not able to hold her course and that her steering gear was damaged. It might still be possible to intercept her. Hope shone out anew.

The Commander-in-Chief turned at once (2142/26) to south hoping to make contact from the eastward in the failing light. At 2228[70] came a signal from Vice-Admiral Somerville reporting that the *Bismarck* had been hit. The weather was as bad as ever. Rain squalls and gathering darkness made the prospect of interception uncertain and the Commander-in-Chief decided to haul off to the eastward and northward and work round to engage from the westward at dawn. He turned eastward at 2306/26 (see Plan 6). Reports began to come in steadily from the destroyers confirming the *Bismarck's* northerly course. They were some distance off to the south-eastward, though their exact position was not easy to determine on account of the differences of reckoning arising from widely separated forces operating far apart in bad weather. At 0236/27 the Commander-in-Chief ordered Captain (D) 4th Flotilla to fire star-shell every half hour, but frequent rain squalls prevented their being seen and they tended to attract the enemy's fire. The *Bismarck* was still a formidable opponent for at 0353/27 Captain D reported that she had done 8 miles in the last hour and was still capable of heavy and accurate fire. On account of the uncertainty of the relative positions and poor visibility, the Commander-in-Chief decided not to make a dawn approach but to wait for full light, approaching from the westward "with the advantages of wind, sea, and light". At 0529 the *Rodney* reported the *Norfolk* to the eastward by D.F. It was light at 0600. Day dawned out of a leaden sky lowering over a rising sea and heavy swell. A tearing wind from the north-west. At 0820 the *Norfolk* is seen on the port bow. She signals "Enemy, 130°, 16 miles." "On tin hats!" At 0843 looming on the starboard bow there emerges out of a rain squall the dark grey blot of a large ship. "Enemy in sight."

The *Bismarck*

The *Bismarck* after altering course to the north-west at about 2300/26 had been labouring along with a jammed rudder, steering an erratic course at about eight knots. The destroyers attacking in the dark were met with heavy and accurate salvoes. Sixteen torpedoes were fired at her. Early in the morning a glare of star-shell burst over her, lighting her up. Three torpedoes followed from a destroyer on the port bow (the *Maori)* of which one hit[71] on the port side amidships. Three minutes later three more came from the starboard side (the *Cossack)* of which one hit on the starboard bow. The nature and extent of the damage sustained is not known. The *Bismarck* lay stopped for over an hour. At 0140 came a message that a large number of Junkers were coming to her help and that U-boats had been ordered to close. She was beyond their help. The aircraft did not find her. One submarine[72] on its way back from the Atlantic joined her and was within sight of her during the night. Another arrived at 0600/27 but it had been damaged in a depth charge attack and could do nothing. In the *Bismarck* the men were exhausted and falling asleep at their posts. It was under these ominous conditions that at about 0840/27 the British battleships were sighted approaching from the westward.

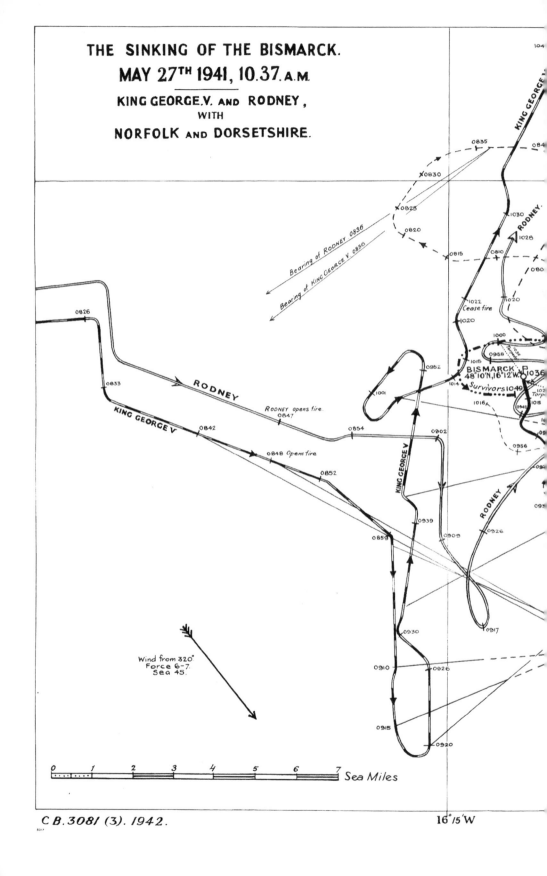

THE SINKING OF THE BISMARCK.
MAY 27TH 1941, 10.37.A.M.
KING GEORGE.V. AND RODNEY,
WITH
NORFOLK AND DORSETSHIRE.

Bearing of RODNEY 0836

Bearing of KING GEORGE V. 0836

RODNEY opens fire.
0847

0848 Opens fire

RODNEY

KING GEORGE V

KING GEORGE V

RODNEY

1022
Cease fire

BISMARCK
48°10'N,16°12'W.
Survivors 1049.

Wind from 320°
Force 6-7.
Sea 45.

0 1 2 3 4 5 6 7 Sea Miles

C B. 3081 (3). 1942.

16°15'W

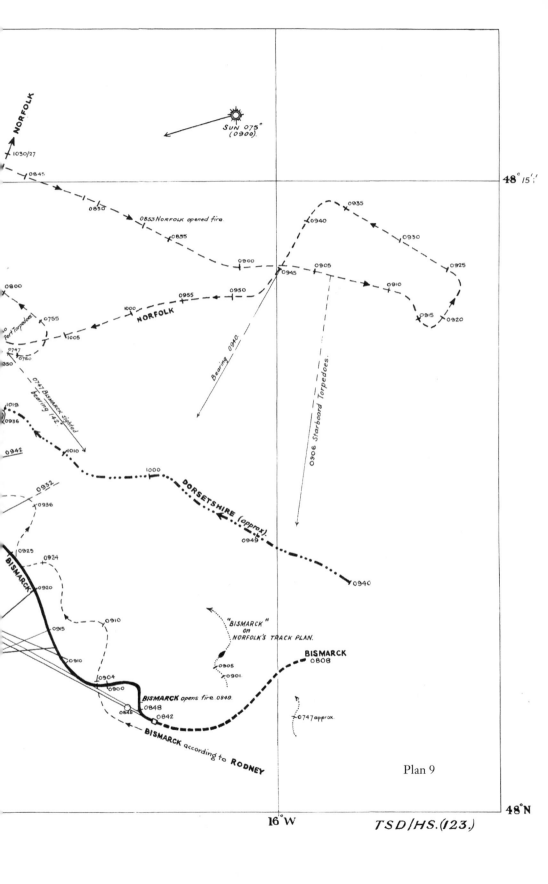

NORFOLK

SUN 075°
(0900).

1030/27

0845

0850

0853 *Norfolk opened fire.*

0855

0900

0945

0935

0940

0930

0925

0905

0910

0915

0920

0800

0755

Port Torpedoes

0955

1000

0950

NORFOLK

1005

0747

0750

350

0741 Bismarck Sighted.
Bearing 142°.

Bearing 0940.

0906 Starboard Torpedoes

1019

0936

0942

1010

1000

0932

0936

DORSETSHIRE *(approx).*

0949

0940

BISMARCK

0925

0924

0920

0910

0915

0910

0904

0900

0846

0848

0842

BISMARCK opens fire. 0849.

"BISMARCK"
on
NORFOLK'S TRACK PLAN.

0905

0901

BISMARCK
0808

0747 *approx.*

BISMARCK *according to* RODNEY

Plan 9

48° 15′

48°N

16°W

TSD/HS.(123.)

The Action
(Plan 9)

Situation Prior to Action

A north-westerly gale was blowing when dawn broke with a good light and clear horizon to the north-eastward. Reports received during the night indicated that, despite reduced speed and damaged rudders, the *Bismarck*'s armament was functioning effectively. The Commander-in-Chief remarks that the strong wind and heavy sea made fighting to windward most undesirable. He therefore decided to approach on a west-north-westerly bearing and, if the enemy maintained his northerly course, to deploy to the southward on opposite courses at about 15,000 yards. Subsequent action was to be dictated by events.

Between 0600 and 0700 a series of enemy reports from the *Maori*, which was herself located by D.F. bearings, enabled the position of the *King George V* to be plotted relatively to the *Bismarck* which had apparently settled down to a course of 330°, 10 knots. At 0708 the *Rodney* was ordered to keep station 6 cables or more and to adjust her own bearings as she liked. Course was altered to 080° at 0737 and the *Rodney* took up station 010° from the Flagship. The *Norfolk* came in sight to the eastward at 0820 and provided a visual link between the Commander-in-Chief and the enemy. After the line of approach had been adjusted by two alterations of course, the *Bismarck* was sighted at 0843 bearing 118°, about 25,000 yards. The British battleships were then steering 110° almost directly towards her in a line abreast formation, 8 cables apart. The tracks of the ships engaged in the subsequent action are shown on Plan 9.

Commencement of Action

The *Rodney* opened fire at 0847, her first salvo sending a column of water 150 ft. into the air. The *King George V* followed a minute later. The *Bismarck* replied at 0850 after turning to open A arcs. The first German salvo was short.[73] The third or fourth (at 0851) straddled and nearly hit, but the *Rodney* manoeuvred successfully to avoid them and the nearest shot fell 20 yards short. Her Captain remarks that the complete freedom of action allowed to him by the Commander-in-Chief facilitated this action. The *Norfolk*, which was flank marking[74] 22,000 yards to the northward, joined in at 0854 but the target was not clearly visible and she opened fire without obtaining a range.

Observers state that the German gunnery was accurate at first, but commenced to deteriorate after 8 or 10 salvoes. Our own hits were difficult to identify owing to the use of armour-piercing shell, but the first one is reported to have been scored at 0854 by the *Rodney*'s third salvo.[75] Both British battleships made small alterations of course away from the enemy shortly after opening fire, the *King George V* to increase her distance from the *Rodney* and the latter to open her A arcs. Thenceforward they manoeuvred independently although the *Rodney* conformed to the Flagship's general movements. The *Bismarck*'s secondary armament came into action during this phase and the *Rodney*'s joined in at 0858.

Run to the Southward

The *King George V* deployed to the southward at 0859 when the *Bismarck* was 16,000 yards distant. The *Rodney*, 2½ miles to the northward, followed suit a minute or two later. Cordite smoke was hanging badly with the following wind and spotting was most difficult. Considerable smoke interference was therefore experienced on the southerly course which was partly overcome by R.D.F. The *Bismarck* had transferred her fire to the *King George V* shortly after the turn but except for an occasional splash the latter hardly knew that she was under fire. At 0902 the *Rodney* saw a 16-in. shell hit the *Bismarck* on the upper deck forward, apparently putting the fore turrets out of action. At 0904 the *Dorsetshire* joined in the firing from the eastward at a range of 20,000 yards but observation of the target was difficult and she had to check fire from 0913 to 0920. Between 0910 and 0915 the range in *King George V* was more or less steady at 12,000 yards.

The fate of the *Bismarck* was decided during this phase of the action although she did not sink until later. Kapitänleutnant von Müllenheim-Rechberg[76] seems to think that she could have held her own if the fore control position had not been hit 25 minutes after the action commenced (i.e., about 0912). The wish must be regarded as father to the thought for the issue had been decided much earlier by the greater volume and accuracy of the British gunfire. Incidentally, the same informant, who was rescued by the *Dorsetshire*, credits her with the alleged lucky shot despite her long range and the inherent improbability of identifying shots from particular ships. During the run to the south, the *Rodney* fired six torpedoes at 11,000 yards and the *Norfolk* four at 16,000 yards,[77] none of which hit. The *King George's* secondary battery which came into action at 0905 increased the smoke interference and was accordingly ordered to cease fire two or three minutes later.

Run to the North

At 0916 the *Bismarck's* bearing was drawing rapidly aft and the *Rodney* turned 16 points to close and head her off. The *King George V* turned a minute or so later and both ships re-opened fire to starboard at ranges of 8,600 and 12,000 respectively. The *Bismarck* shifted her target to the *Rodney* about this time for several shots fell close to the latter and a near miss damaged the sluice door of her starboard torpedo tube. Most of the enemy's guns had however been silenced by then and only "X" turret (i.e., German "C") and part of the secondary armament appeared to be firing. A fire was blazing amidships and she had a heavy list to port. During the run to the north the *Rodney* obtained a very favourable position on the *Bismarck's* bow from which she poured in a heavy fire at comparatively short range. She also fired two torpedoes at 7,500 yards but no hits were obtained.

The *King George's* position further to leeward was less favourable. Her view was obscured by smoke and splashes surrounding the target and her R.D.F. had temporarily broken down. Mechanical failures in the 14-in. turrets constituted however a more serious handicap at this stage. "A", "Y" and "B" turrets were out of action for 30, and 7 minutes, and for a short unspecified period, respectively. This corresponded to a reduction in fire power of 80 per cent. for 7 minutes and 40 per cent. for 23 minutes which might have had serious results under less favourable conditions. There were also several breakdowns of individual guns in addition to those affecting the turrets.

At 0925, the *King George V* altered outwards 150° and reduced speed to avoid getting too far ahead of the target. She closed in again at 1005, fired several salvoes from about 3,000 yards and then resumed her northerly course. Meanwhile the *Rodney* was zigzagging across the *Bismarck's* line of advance at a range of about 4,000 yards, firing her main and secondary armaments. She also fired four torpedoes, one of which was regarded as a hit. By 1015 the *Bismarck* was a wreck. All her guns were silenced, her mast had been blown away; she lay wallowing in the Atlantic swell – a black ruin, pouring high into the air a great cloud of smoke and flame. Men were seen jumping overboard at this time and the Captain of the *King George V* remarks that had he known it he would have ceased fire.

Signal sent to Fleet Commander

0153/27 I thank you in the name of the German people.

Adolf Hitler

Signal sent to the crew of battleship *Bismarck*

0153/27 The whole of Germany is with you. What can still be done will be done. The performance of your duty will strengthen our people in the struggle for their existence.

Adolf Hitler

Signal sent from *Bismarck* to C.-in-C., Navy

0221/27 Propose Lt. Cdr. Schneider (Gunnery Officer) be awarded Knights Cross for sinking *Hood*.

Fleet Commander

Signal sent to Lt. Cdr. Schneider

0351/27 The Führer has awarded you the Knights Cross for sinking the battlecruiser *Hood*. Heartiest congratulations.

C.-in-C., Navy

Signal sent from *Bismarck* to Group West

0710/27 Send U-boat to save War Diary.

Fleet Commander
(This was the last signal made by *Bismarck*)

Signal sent to Fleet Commander

1322/27 Reuter reports: *Bismarck* sunk. Report situation immediately.

Group West

End of Action

The Commander-in-Chief was confident that the enemy could never get back to harbour, and as the battleships were running short of fuel and as further gunfire was unlikely to hasten the *Bismarck*'s end, the Commander-in-Chief signalled the *King George V* and *Rodney* to steer 027° at 1015 in order to break off the action and return to their base. At 1036, he directed the *Dorsetshire* to use her torpedoes, if she had any, on the enemy. In the meantime, the *Norfolk* had been closing the target but owing to the movements of the *King George V* and *Rodney*, had withheld her torpedoes until 1010 when four were fired at 4,000 yards and two possible hits were reported. The *Dorsetshire* was then approaching a mile or so to the southward, and anticipating the Commander-in-Chief's signal at 1025 fired two torpedoes at 3,600 yards into the enemy's starboard side. One exploded under the forebridge and the other is thought to have struck further aft. She then steamed round the *Bismarck*'s bow and at 1036 fired another torpedo into her port side at a range of 2,600 yards. This was the final blow; the great German battleship heeled over quickly to port and commenced to sink by the stern. The hull turned over keel up and disappeared at 1040.

The *Dorsetshire* closed and signalled to one of the *Ark Royal*'s aircraft to carry out a close submarine patrol whilst she picked up survivors, at the same time directing the *Maori* to assist in this difficult task. The ship was rolling heavily in a very steep sea, but rafts, buoys, hawsers and life lines were thrown over the side. After about 80 men had been hauled onboard, a suspicious smoky discharge was observed about 2 miles away on the leeward beam. In view of this and other indications that hostile aircraft and submarines were probably in the vicinity,[78] the *Dorsetshire* reluctantly left the scene of the sinking. A total of 110 survivors including four officers were picked up by the *Dorsetshire* and *Maori*. A further 100 are said to have been picked up by the German fishing vessel *Sachsenwald*, operating as a weather reporting ship from Bordeaux. The Spanish cruiser *Canarias* also proceeded to the spot but found only floating bodies.

Damage to *Bismarck*

Survivors have told the story of terrible damage inflicted on her. The fore turrets seem to have been knocked out at 0902; the fore control position was knocked out about 0912; the after control position followed about 0915. The after turrets were still in action. Then the after turret (D turret) is said to have been disabled by a direct hit on the left gun, which burst sending a flash right through the turret. C turret was the last in action.

One survivor states that at 0930 a shell penetrated the turbine room and another entered the boiler room. A hit in the after dressing station killed all the medical staff and wounded in it. The upper deck was crowded with killed and wounded and the seas surging in washed them overboard. Conditions below were still more terrible. Hatches and doors were jammed by concussion and blocked with wreckage. The air was thick with smoke and fumes of shell; smoke was pouring from great holes in the upper deck, six feet wide. By 1000/27 her heavy guns were completely out of action though her secondary guns kept up a spasmodic fire. By 1010 they too were silent.[79]

Commander-in-Chief Returns

As the *King George V* and *Rodney* turned northward they were joined by the *Cossack*, *Sikh* and *Zulu* and by 1600/28, eleven more had joined the screen. Heavy air attacks were expected that day, but only four enemy planes appeared, one of which bombed the screen, while another jettisoned its bombs on being attacked by a Blenheim fighter. The destroyers *Mashona* and *Tartar*, some 100 miles to the southward, were not so fortunate. They were attacked by aircraft at 0955/28 in 52° 58' N., 11° 36' W., about 100 miles west of Galway, and the *Mashona* was hit and sank at noon with the loss of 1 officer and 45 men. The Commander-in-Chief reached Loch Ewe at 1230/29; Vice-Admiral Somerville and Force H were on their way back to Gibraltar. Such were the operations associated with the destruction of the *Bismarck*, which the Commander-in-Chief sums up as follows in his despatch:–

"Although it was no more than I expected, the co-operation, skill and understanding displayed by all forces during this prolonged chase gave me the utmost satisfaction. Flag and Commanding Officers of detached units invariably took the action I would have wished, before or without receiving instructions from me. The conduct of all officers and men of the Fleet which I have the honour to command was in accordance with the tradition of the Service. Force H was handled with conspicuous skill throughout the operation by Vice-Admiral Sir James F. Somerville, K.C.B., D.S.O., and contributed a vital share in its successful conclusion. The accuracy of the enemy information supplied by the Admiralty and the speed with which it was passed were remarkable and the balance struck between information and instructions passed to the forces out of visual touch with me, was ideal."[80]

Submarines Off Brest

The *Prinz Eugen* was not heard of again till 4 June when aircraft reported her in Brest. At 1244/25, six submarines[81] had been ordered to take up position about 120 miles west of Brest. They were ordered to move their patrol to the south-east at 2219/25 when it was thought that the enemy might make for St. Nazaire. On 27 May an enemy cruiser was reported at 1820/27 in 47° N., 14° 30' W.[82] and the patrols, by that time reduced to five (for H 44 had to return) were altered accordingly. Nothing was seen of the *Prinz Eugen*. There can be little doubt that the task allotted to her and the *Bismarck* was associated with a large movement of German supply ships in the Atlantic which was taking place at this time, for between 4 and 23 June no fewer than eight were intercepted by British ships[83] and scuttled themselves or were sunk.

Conclusion

This was one of the most striking events of the war, and perhaps indeed of all the events recorded in British naval history. For it not only covered a very wide area and required the sudden concentration of a great number of dispersed ships, but it was marked by continuous and successive co-operation on the part of all forces concerned. For the pursuit began with cruisers and when the enemy was lost, he was found by aircraft and later was picked up again by a cruiser which in its turn directed the aircraft who struck the fatal blow. And just as the cruiser lost her, destroyers took up the trail and shadowed her through the night. Moreover on no occasion has the value of aircraft been so clearly demonstrated, for it was aircraft that found her when lost and aircraft that made the decisive attack. Nor perhaps has any event presented a picture of more vivid contrasts, for each adversary was tossed in turn between high hope and deep disappointment, between the extreme poles of shining fortune and black mischance. For at first all went well with the new battleship and she achieved a great success. Then came a twin-bolt from the evening sky which brought her to a sudden stop. Following hard behind came the avenging battleships and the great flagship and the admiral and all his plans were sunk.

Appendix A

**Bismarck Operations
List Of H.M. Ships**

A/CC. = Aircraft Carrier.

B. = Battleship.

B.C. = Battlecruiser.

C. = Cruiser.

D. = Destroyer.

Name Of Ship	Description	Main Armament	Commanding Officer
King George V	B.	10 14-in. 16 5.25-in	Captain W. R. Patterson, C.V.O. (Flag of Commander-in-Chief H.F. Admiral J. C. Tovey, K.C.B., D.S.O.).
		First Cruiser Squadron	
Norfolk	C.	8 8-in.	Captain A. J. L. Phillips (Flag of Rear-Admiral, First Cruiser Squadron, Rear-Admiral W. F. Wake-Walker, C.B.).
Suffolk	C.	8 8-in.	Captain R. M. Ellis.
		Second Cruiser Squadron	
Galatea	C.	6 6-in.	Captain E. W. B. Sim (Flag of Rear-Admiral, 2nd Cruiser Squadron, Rear-Admiral A. T. B. Curteis, C.B.).
Aurora	C.	6 6-in.	Captain W. G. Agnew.

Kenya	C.	12 6-in.	Captain M. M. Denny, C.B.
Neptune	C.	8 6-in.	Captain R. C. O'Conor.
Hermione	C.	10 5.25-in.	Captain G. N. Oliver.
Active	D.	4 4.7-in. (Q.F.)	Lieutenant-Commander M. W. Tomkinson.
Punjabi	D.	6 4.7-in.	Commander S. A. Buss, M.V.O.
Nestor	D.	6 4.7-in.	Commander C. B. Alers-Hankey, D.S.C.
Inglefield	D.	5 4.7-in. (Q.F.)	Captain P. Todd, D.S.O. (Captain (D), Third Destroyer Flotilla.)
Intrepid	D.	4 4.7-in. (Q.F.)	Commander R. C. Gordon, D.S.O.
Repulse	B.C.	6 15-in. 9 4-in.	Captain W. G. Tennant, C. B., M.V.O.
Victorious	A/CC.	16 4.5-in.	Captain H. C. Bovell.

Battlecruiser Squadron

Hood	B.C.	8 15-in. 14 4-in. H.A.	Captain R. Kerr, C.B.E. (Flag of Vice-Admiral, Battlecruiser Squadron, Vice-Admiral L. E. Holland, C.B.).
Prince Of Wales	B.	10 14-in. 16 5.25-in.	Captain J. C. Leach, M.V.O.
Electra	D.	4 4.7-in. (Q.F.)	Commander C. W. May.
Anthony	D.	4 4.7-in. (Q.F.)	Lieutenant-Commander J. M. Hodges.
Echo	D.	4 4.7-in. (Q.F.)	Lieutenant-Commander C. H. de B. Newby.

Icarus	D.	4 4.7-in. (Q.F.)	Lieutenant-Commander C. D. Maud, D.S.C.
Achates	D.	4 4.7-in. (Q.F.)	Lieutenant-Commander Viscount Jocelyn.
Antelope	D.	4 4.7-in. (Q.F.)	Lieutenant-Commander R. B. N. Hicks, D.S.O.
Rodney	B.	9 16-in. 12 6-in.	Captain F. H. G. Dalrymple-Hamilton.
Ramillies	B.	8 15-in. 12 6-in.	Captain A. D. Read.
Revenge	B.	8 15-in. 12 6-in.	Captain E. R. Archer.

Force H

Renown	B.C.	6 15-in. 20 4.5-in. H.A.	Captain R. R. McGrigor (Flag of Vice-Admiral, Force H, Vice-Admiral Sir J. F. Somerville, K.C.B., D.S.O.).
Ark Royal	A/CC.	16 4.5-in.	Captain L. E. H. Maund.
Sheffield	C.	12 6-in.	Captain C. A. A. Larcom.
Manchester	C.	12 6-in.	Captain H. A. Packer.
Birmingham	C.	12 6-in.	Captain A. C. G. Madden.
Arethusa	C.	6 6-in.	Captain A. C. Chapman.
Edinburgh	C.	12 6-in.	Commodore C. M. Blackman, D.S.O. (Broad Pendant, Commodore 18th Cruiser Squadron).

London	C.	8 8-in.	Captain R. M. Servaes, C.B.E.
Dorsetshire	C.	8 8-in.	Captain B. C. S. Martin.
Cossack	D.	6 4.7-in.	Captain P. L. Vian, D.S.O. (Captain (D), Fourth Destroyer Flotilla).
Sikh	D.	6 4.7-in.	Commander G. H. Stokes.
Zulu	D.	6 4.7-in.	Commander H. R. Graham, D.S.O.
Maori	D.	6 4.7-in.	Commander H. T. Armstrong, D.S.C.
Piorun (Polish) (Late *Nerissa*)	D.	6 4.7-in.	Commander E. Plawski.
Somali	D.	6 4.7-in.	Captain C. Caslon.
Tartar	D.	6 4.7-in.	Commander L. P. Skipwith.
Mashona	D.	6 4.7-in.	Commander W. H. Selby.
Columbia (Late *Haraden*)	D.	3 4-in.	Lieutenant-Commander S. W. Davis.
Eskimo	D.	6 4.7-in.	Lieutenant J. V. Wilkinson.
Jupiter	D.	6 4.7-in.	Lieutenant-Commander N. V. J. T. Thew.
Minerve[84] (French)	Submarine	Lieutenant de Vaisseau P. M. Sommeville.	
P.31[84]	Submarine	Lieutenant J. B. de B. Kershaw.	

Appendix B

Torpedoes Fired at *Bismarck*

S.S. = Starboard side.
P.S. = Port side.

Unit	Attack Time	No. of torpedoes fired (jettisoned)	Hits	Possible
Victorious	25/2400	8(1)	1 S.S.	
Ark Royal	26/1550 1st (HMS *Sheffield*)	11 (3)		
	26/2100 2nd	13 (2)	1 P.S. 1 S.S.	1
	27/1016 3rd	Nil (15)		
Cossack	27/0140 1st	3	1 S.S.	
	27/0335 2nd	1		
Maori	27/0137 1st	2	1 P.S.	
	27/0656 2nd	2		
Zulu	27/0121	4		
Sikh	27/0128	4		1
Rodney	Action 27 May	12	1 P.S.	
Norfolk	Action 27 May	8		1
Dorsetshire	27/1025	3	1 S.S. 1 P.S.	1
Total fired and expended		71 Fired		
		92 Expended	8	4

Appendix C

Torpedo Attacks by 7th Destroyer Division on *Bismarck*, 27 May, 1941.

Ship	Time	Range	Inclination	Torpedoes	Hits
Zulu	0121	3000	90L	4	
Maori	0137	3400	045L	2	1
Cossack	0140	6000 R.D.F.	100 R	3	1
Sikh	0128	7000 R.D.F.	80-100 L	4	1 (possible)
Cossack	0335	4000 R.D.F.	170 L	1	
Maori	0656	9000	90 R	2	

Appendix D

The following ammunition was expended during the action, 27 May:–

Ship	16-in.	14-in.	8-in.	6-in.	5.25-in.	Torpedoes
King George V		339			660	
Rodney	380			716		12
Norfolk			527			8
Dorsetshire			254			3
	380	339	881	716	660	23

Endnotes

1. Up to 31 May, 1941, out of 6,803,807 tons gross sunk (British, Allied and Neutral), 911,812 tons (or 13.5 per cent.) were sunk by raiders.
2. N.A. Stockholm 2058/20.
3. 60° 19' N., 5° 14' E. Air alarm in *Bismarck* 1330/21.
4. Between Iceland and Greenland.
5. It carried Commander G. A. Rotherham, R.N., an observer of much experience, and was piloted by Lieut. (A) N. N. Goddard, R.N.V.R.
6. At 1928, opened fire, three salvoes (survivors). Note: *Bismarck*'s time was 1 hour behind British.
7. There is no record of this signal having been passed to the two cruisers, nor was it received by them.
8. Fire at left-hand German ship bearing 337°.
9. "Shift object one right." There is no record as to whether the *Prince of Wales'* guns were actually laid on the *Prinz Eugen*. The silhouettes of the *Bismarck* and *Prinz Eugen* were very similar.
10. Two guns of the four in the after turret were ready for action by 0720. (*Prince of Wales'* report.)
11. Reports from *Prince of Wales, Echo, Icarus, Achates, Malcolm* and Flag Officer, Iceland. The *Anthony* and *Antelope* had been detached by the *Hood* to Iceland to fuel at 1400/23. When the report of the enemy came in on 23 May, they were ordered by Flag Officer, Iceland, to join the 1st B.C.S. and sailed at 2100/23. Four destroyers remained with *Hood* (*Echo, Electra, Icarus, Achates*). They had difficulty in maintaining station in the heavy sea when the *Hood* went on to 27 knots at 2054/23. At 2120/23 Rear-Admiral 1st B.C.S. signalled his intention to spread destroyers 70° 7 miles apart at 2300. At 2318/23 destroyers were ordered to form screen No. 4 (i.e., ahead). At 2359/23 the *Hood* turned to North. At 0147/24 destroyers were told that if battlecruisers turned to 200° they were to continue to northward. It is clear that they did continue to the northward for when the action started at 0555/24 they were all some 30 miles to the northward or north-westward. At 0637/24 they were ordered by Rear-Admiral 1st Cruiser Squadron to search for survivors. They reached the scene of the explosion about 0745/24. It was marked by a large patch of oil, wreckage, hammocks, Balsa rafts, splinters and charred wood. Only three survivors were picked up (by the *Electra*). The *Malcolm* arrived from Iceland and was searching all day without result. She reported the scene of the disaster to be in 63° 14' N., 32° 22' W. The *Echo* reports that she with the *Icarus, Achates, Antelope* and *Anthony* proceeded at 0900/24 to Hvalfjord to fuel, arriving at 2000/24.
12. Later 600 tons.
13. Four guns of the after turret were unserviceable from 0613 to 0720 and two guns up to 0825.
14. Later 26 knots.
15. At 1917/24 ordered to overtake convoy HX128 from Halifax.
16. My position 0800, 61° 17' N., 22° 8' W., closing you at 27 knots.
17. Apparently not sighted in *Bismarck*.

18. R.A.C.S. 1 to Admiralty 1619/24.
19. The *Prince of Wales* 1847/24; *Norfolk* 1853/24.
20. The *Victorious* and 2nd C.S. had parted company from the Commander-in-Chief at 1509/24.
21. The *London* had previously been escorting *Arundel Castle* from Gibraltar.
22. Left Halifax 1505/24. H X 128 (44 ships) at 0800/24 was in 42° 54' N., 50° 8' W., steaming 95° 6½ knots.
23. The *Edinburgh* (18th C.S.) left Scapa on 18 May to patrol between 44° N. and 46° N. for enemy merchant ships. She had intercepted German S.S. *Lechs* on 22 May.
24. Course 240°; position of *Victorious* at 1600, 59° 47' N., 28° 42' W.
25. One had lost contact in the cloud.
26. Commander-in-Chief's despatch, paragraph 37.
27. A survivor mentioned the *Prinz Eugen* as leaving at 0509/24. This is evidently much too early, though she may possibly have increased her distance at that time.
28. Believed to be the *Modoc*.
29. The *Prince of Wales* says "three flashes"; Rear-Admiral 1st Cruiser Squadron says "two salvoes".
30. "The loss of touch, when it came, was caused primarily by over-confidence. The R.D.F. had been giving such consistently good results and had been used so skilfully that it engendered a false sense of security . . . The *Suffolk* was shadowing from the extreme range of her instrument, losing touch on those parts of her zigzag which took her furthest from the enemy. The enemy altered sharply to starboard, while the *Suffolk* was moving to port, and by the time she got back had gone." (Commander-in-Chief's despatch. Par. 45. C.B. 04164, page 18.)
31. Received in *Norfolk* 0445/25.
32. This was considerably to the south-west of his actual position.
33. F.O. Force H gives position at 0330/25 as 39° 35' N., 14° 10' W., steering 310° at 24 knots.
34. Commander-in-Chief's despatch, paragraph 52. A first set of bearings of signals made by enemy at 0654/25 was sent out by Admiralty at 0927/25 and was received in *King George V* at 1010/25. A second set made at 0748/25 went out at 1030/25 and was received at 1106/25. (*King George V*'s signal log.)
35. The *Bismarck* seems to have been actually some 60 miles to the southward.
36. The *Victorious* lost two Fulmars on 24/25 May and two Swordfish during searches on 25/26 May. One landed alongside a ship's lifeboat, empty, but stored with provisions and water; the crew were nine days in her before being rescued by a merchant vessel. (Commander-in-Chief, paragraph 56.)
37. "Proceed on assumption enemy turned towards Brest." Received *Norfolk* 1045/25.
38. From Commander-in-Chief's track chart. The Admiralty plotted her by D.F. bearings at 1054/25 in approximately 55° 30' N, and between 31° and 32° W. (Signal to Commander-in-Chief 1228/25, received in *King George V* at 1401/25.) (See Plan 6.)
39. Commander-in-Chief's despatch, paragraph 53.
40. i.e., of 1047/25 to search towards the D.F. position of 0852/25 in 57° N. 33° W.
41. Flown off 2110/25; landed on 0005/26.
42. Commander-in-Chief to Admiralty, 2238/25.
43. Through 50° 10' N., 21° W.; 52° 20' N., 19° 25' W.; 48° 10' N., 23° 30' W.; 49° 50' N., 21° 10' W. First Sea Lord 0109/26.
44. The *Cossack* (Captain Philip Vian), *Maori*, *Zulu*, *Sikh*, and (Polish) *Piorun*.
45. An air reconnaissance of Brest made by Plymouth at 1930/25 had reported the battlecruisers still there. This went out from the Admiralty at 2108/25 and was passed to Gibraltar for the *Renown*. It was received at Gibraltar 2226/25. The *Renown* however had shifted to Home wave at 0034/26. (M.09199/41.)

46. 56 ft.
47. One battleship, bearing 240° 5 miles, course 150°, my position 49° 33' N. 21° 47' W. 1030/26.
48. By Flag Officer, Force H at 1050/26.
49. One of the *Ark Royal* planes reported the ship sighted as a cruiser.
50. The Catalinas regained touch at 1330/26.
51. Lands End, 638 miles 87°; Finisterre, 675 miles, 125°.
52. First reconnaissance to 1250; first relief 1230-1553, 12 reports; second relief 1624-1850, 9 reports; third relief 1900-2130, 7 reports. (Force H, signal log).
53. The *Bismarck* survivor's diary C.B. 4051 (24) page 57 "0700/26. Enemy squadron in sight in the distance." Note that German 0700 = British 0800.
54. The report to Admiralty at 1345 that *Sheffield* had been detached had been received in *Ark Royal* but had not been decoded, when striking force left; *Ark Royal* made a warning signal to aircraft at 1620/26.
55. Fifteen flew off, one returned immediately.
56. A Catalina reported her at 1500/26 in 47° 30' N. 19° W. which would make her some 82 miles south of the *Sheffield*. The same Catalina (M.240) was in visual touch with the Sheffield at 1740/26, and gave its own position at 1800/26 as 47° 15' N. 18° 23' W. some 62 miles south of the *Sheffield's* (see Plan 6).
57. The *Ark Royal's* report gives two hits and one probable. *Ark Royal* to Flag Officer, Force H, at 2213/26, "one hit amidships"; at 2240/26 "possible second hit on starboard quarter".
58. Eight aircraft had been up, shadowing all day two at a time. "Their work throughout the day was particularly well carried out." (*Ark Royal's* report in C.B. 04164, page 50, paragraph 35.)
59. Survivors' reports. It is difficult to fit this into the *Bismarck's* track.
60. Presumably about 2100/26.
61. Sunset was at 2248 (Midsummer Time). Nautical Twilight (i.e., up to 12° below horizon) ended at 0020, 27 May. There was no moon.
62. As things turned out, the *Cossack* and *Maori* were able to fire torpedoes from opposite sides of the *Bismarck* within three minutes of each other.
63. The *Maori's* report. This does not agree with position of *Maori* and *Sikh* at this time as shown in plan 8, drawn from the tactical plot accompanying Capt. D.4's report. The *Maori's* report is quite definite: "At about 0020/27, *Bismarck* opened fire on *Sikh* . . . *Bismarck* was then bearing 330° from *Maori*, steering approximately 320°. *Maori* was close on *Sikh's* beam. At 0025 salvoes started falling very close to both ships . . ."
64. See Appendix C.
65. The *Piorun* appears also to have been in this vicinity. As there is no record of her track, and the report subsequently received from her contains very few times, it is not possible to state what her actual movements were.
66. In the excitement of the moment, the rating operating the torpedo-firing levers fired without any appreciable spread and with scarcely any interval between the torpedoes. An underwater explosion, however, was heard in the engine room at about the right time for a hit on the enemy.
67. Sunrise was at 0712 B.S.T. Nautical twilight commenced at 0542.
68. In his report to the Commander-in-Chief, Captain Vian makes the following remarks in connection with this order:– "She was short of fuel. She had, with great intrepidity, continued to close the enemy in daylight after first sighting, going into action with her 4.7-in. guns. She had been unable to find the enemy to attack him during the night, and I knew Commander Plawski would certainly go for him as soon as he could find him; conditions as light came on would not be easy, and I was concerned lest a valuable ship and a fine crew should be lost without need. I had no doubt the 7th division unassisted could deliver the enemy to you."

69. Sunrise at 0722.
70. From F.O., Force H 2225/26 (received 2228/26), "one hit"; 2240/26 "possible second hit".
71. Possibly two, see Survivors' reports, C.B. 4051 (24) page 20.
72. This submarine was sunk by destroyers on 27 June. The information is from her survivors. They stated also that she was within 218 yards of the *King George V* but had no torpedoes available. A submarine was detected by HMS *Norfolk* at 0508/27 in 48° 26' N., 15° 18' W.
73. The *Rodney* says 1,000 yards and the *King George V* 400.
74. No flank marking signals were received in *King George V* (H.F. Gunnery report, paragraph 26).
75. The *Bismarck*'s survivors say that she was first hit at 0857 but little reliance can be placed on their times. *Vide* Interrogation of Survivors, C.B. 4051 (24).
76. The *Vide* Interrogation of Survivors, C.B. 4051 (24), page 22.
77. According to the track chart her distance was 21,000 yards at 0906.
78. See S.35, footnote.
79. For further details and particulars of *Bismarck* see Survivors reports, C.B. 4051 (24), 1941.
80. Commander-in-Chief despatch, paragraphs 92 and 93.
81. H 44, *Sea Lion*, *Seawolf*, *Pandora*, *Sturgeon* and *Tigris*.
82. i.e., in about the position of Bismarck at 2400/26.
83. 4 June, *Esso Hamburg* by HMS *London*; 4 June, German tanker by *Marsdale*; 4 June, *Gonzenheim* by *Neptune*; 5 June, tanker *Egerland* by *London*; 12 June, tanker *Friedrich Breme* by *Sheffield*; 21 June, *Babitonga* by *London*; *Elbe* by *Hilary*; 23 June, *Alstertor*.
84. Off Norway.

Part III

Personal Accounts

Extract from the Memoir of R. J. Jandrell DSM

I went home from work one day and was asked by my sister if I would put her name and address in a box on an export tin plate, as she wanted a pen pal. I did as she asked and sure enough, after a while, she had a letter from a Betty Jane Donart. After exchanging a few letters, she asked my sister if she could put her friend, Jackie Browning, in touch with a young man – my sister passed her address on to me. This was my first contact with the United States of America. Little did I think, at the time, what an experience this was going to lead to. I may add that we are still in contact with Jackie – only now it is my wife who writes!

On 4 June 1940, like so many others of my age, I joined the Royal Navy as an engine room artificer, and after a very brief course in naval engineering and a briefer period of training, on 4 July I joined HMS *Rodney*. *Rodney*, at that time, was the largest battleship afloat – 42,000 tons and a complement of 1,600 men.

My first trip was convoy duty from Scapa Flow to Halifax, Nova Scotia, patrolling in the North Atlantic for about 30 days. It was on this first trip that we had a call from the *Jervis Bay* action but we were unable to arrive in time and the *Jervis Bay* was sunk. We spent the next few months based at Reykjavik, Iceland, covering every convoy to and from England – there were usually 200 ships in a convoy.

At this period, the *Scharnhorst*, *Gneisenau* and the German Pocket Battleships were operating in the Atlantic, as well as armed merchant ships, and it was our job to keep these enemy ships away from our vital convoys – and if they did come anywhere near us, chase, engage and sink them.

After about six months on this duty and a few trips ashore at Halifax where prohibition was on and at Reykjavik where we didn't have a very friendly reception, we were pleased to hear that we were making for Greenock – which meant a trip ashore at Glasgow. After about a week, all leave was stopped and we were told that we would be escorting the most important convoy of the war. This consisted of the liners *Queen Elizabeth* and *Queen Mary*. Both the ships were full of young men chosen to go to Canada to train as pilots, thus enabling us to have the 1,000 bomber raids later on in the war.

Aboard our ship were all the VIPs connected with the convoy – high ranking officers, training officers, American naval and army officers and many others who had to get to Canada safely. With these extra 500 onboard, our complement was over 2,000.

On 22 May 1941, we left the Clyde with our two ships and after two days at sea we had orders from the Admiralty to stay at the stern of the convoy as the *Bismarck* had been reported in the Denmark Straits and was obviously after our convoy. The next information we had was that the *Hood* and the *Prince of Wales* were going to intercept the *Bismarck* – then shortly afterwards the news came that they had sighted the *Bismarck* and were going to engage. The *Hood*, to the Royal Navy, was the pride of the Fleet, while the *Prince of Wales* was new and untried, but we knew she was fast and powerful and our thoughts were, "That's the end of the *Bismarck*".

You can imagine the ship's company's feeling when, not very long afterwards, our Captain broadcast to us that the *Bismarck* had sunk the *Hood* with only a few survivors, and the *Prince of Wales* was hit and put out of action. About 1,600 sailors were killed in the action. I remember well the gloom over the whole ship and a determination in everyone, no matter what branch they were in, to do everything in their power to avenge the sinking of the *Hood* and the damage done to our newest battleship. On the other hand, we couldn't help wondering what new methods of gunnery or what sort of gunnery tables they had to put two such fine ships out of action – and if we should engage this ship, just what we could expect.

Our Captain at this time was F. H. G. Dalrymple-Hamilton and he decided our only course was to get between the *Bismarck* and the French coast, which, he thought, she would make for if things got too hot for her. The only thing we lacked was speed, so our Captain signalled that the *Bismarck* had to be slowed down. This was done by the Swordfish planes of the *Ark Royal* which torpedoed the *Bismarck* in the stern, putting one propeller out of action and damaging the rudder.

The cruiser, *Sheffield*, which was shadowing the *Bismarck*, signalled she was "Changing course towards the French coast", which proved our Captain's theory and we were now closing in on the *Bismarck*. Our Captain told the ship's company that if the engine room staff could get a few more knots out of the old ship, we would be in range by nightfall. This we did, getting 23 knots out of a ship – this had never been done before. When she was pushed her limit was never more than 20 knots and our normal full speed was about 18 knots.

At 2am on Tuesday 27 May, we sighted the *Bismarck*, but we had orders from the Commander-in-Chief aboard the *King George V* that there was to be no night attack. What our Captain had to ensure was that when the dawn broke, the *Bismarck* had to be silhouetted on the horizon where the sun was rising, enabling us to fire the first salvo. This we did, and we opened fire at 8.50am, the *Rodney* hitting the *Bismarck* with the third salvo at a range of 22 miles. This, I think, was remarkable gunnery and an all time record. The *Bismarck*'s first salvo fell 1,000 yards short, the second salvo straddled us and the third was only 20 yards short – we had shrapnel holes in our upper structures and lower decks.

The *Bismarck* fired intermittently, with X turret having several near misses, one of which put the sluice valve door of our torpedo tube out of action. We hit her repeatedly with 16-inch salvo and later with 6-inch shells and at least one torpedo. Forty minutes after the start of the action her guns were silenced and at 10.10am she sank, after being torpedoed several times by the destroyer, *Dorsetshire*.

An experience such as this is something one can never forget. It certainly was the longest 40 minutes of my life and I can assure you, no one has heard a noise until they have heard nine 16-inch guns going off at the same time.

Conditions in the engine room and boiler room were almost unbearable, the temperature in the engine room being 110 degrees and 120 degrees in the boiler room. One boiler was repaired when the temperature was 124 degrees – this is down on record.

Every time we fired a nine gun salvo we had to decide among ourselves if we had been hit or not. Then the Padre would announce over our speaker that another salvo had been fired and whether it had hit its target or not. It was feeling of relief to us when the Padre announced that we had, at last, silenced the *Bismarck*'s guns and we were now breaking off the engagement. I was in the starboard forward engine room during the whole of the engagement. We, in the engine room, took turns to climb up the fan trunking which was our escape hatch from the engine room, to have our first and only look at the sinking *Bismarck*. What I saw made me feel very sad and yet thankful. The *Bismarck* was blazing from stem to stern and as far as the eye could see there were German sailors on rafts and in the water: a sight which could so easily have been reversed.

After the sinking of the *Bismarck*, we expected, and had, quite a lot of excitement. The Germans knew our position and ordered all conceivable submarines and planes to that area. The Admiralty in turn had ordered all available destroyers to escort us and the *King George V* back to Greenock. The RAF supplied air cover and until dark we had a few very hectic hours.

Our destroyer screen systematically threw depth charges to keep the submarines well below and every time these went off, the noise and vibration were terrific. In fact, we often thought that we must have been hit by a torpedo. Our planes gave us very good air cover, but even so, some of the enemy planes did get through. When this happened we would fire what was called a Box Barrage. This means all AA guns form a box shape over the ship making it almost impossible for enemy planes to penetrate and get in a position to bomb us. This form of defence was later used extensively in the Malta convoys.

Later that evening, fortunately, there was a storm, making it impossible for more enemy planes to take off, also for subs to operate, and we arrived at Greenock quite safely.

The ship's company were now looking forward to some shore leave, which we thought we deserved, and it was with a feeling of great apprehension that we heard we would still have to go to the United States of America for a refit as the only two docks in the UK that could take us, Rosyth and Plymouth, were not available.

As it was impracticable to keep a full ship's company out of the war for a long period, it was decided to keep what is known as a 'morale party' onboard. Their job being to keep the ship under supervision while on dockyard hands – and to behave themselves when ashore. I was one of the fortunate ones chosen to stay onboard, but I didn't think so at the time.

After commissioning the ship once again, we sailed for Boston, Massachusetts, calling first at Halifax, Nova Scotia, with the VIPs whom we still had to deliver safely across the Atlantic. They all had an experience which I feel sure they would never forget. Incidentally, the 'Queens' arrived at Halifax safely.

It was a wonderful sight and experience for me, a wartime sailor, to be on a British battleship entering a foreign port with all the pomp and tradition that only the Royal Navy can pull off. Everyone off-duty was on deck in their best uniform, with the Marine band playing traditional British tunes on the forecastle, and in the evening I saw something which was new to me – lights from ashore. As you know, England was blacked out and I had never seen a town or city, in fact any lights at all while onboard ship. All the ship's company, except the morale party, embarked and sailed to England and home leave. My only thought as they sailed off was, "I wish I were with them".

We docked, and at about 6pm we went ashore to have what was, for most of us, our first glimpse of America. When we arrived at the dockyard gates we had our first experience of American hospitality. There was quite a crowd of American people with their cars, some inviting us to their homes and some out for dinner and entertainment. My friend and I went off with a jeweller, Mr. John J. Stannish, and he proved to be a wonderful friend and Samaritan during our four-month stay in Boston. We both had a key to his home, to come and go when we liked, and he was emphatic that we weren't to sleep onboard ship while we were in Boston – our beds were always ready for us.

Every evening we went ashore, we were taken out by all types and nationalities. We had a wonderful time and it didn't cost us a cent. My pay as Chief Petty Officer was about $80 a month. This could easily have been spent in a week, so we had to depend on what we called our 'Barons' for our free entertainment and eats.

I did have one source of income there. When we were particularly 'short', my friends and I would put all our money together, go to a Pool room, then wait until we were challenged to a game. My chums would say, "He's the only one who plays." So the challenger would usually say, "Have a game, Limey?" Limey is the name the Americans call us Britishers. The Americans always play for a dollar a game, doubling up every game they lose. So I had to make sure to win – but not by a great margin, thus enabling my opponent to play another game, not liking to be beaten by a 'Limey'. When I had won enough, and there were no more challengers in the room, we would go out with quite a few dollars, enough anyhow to tide us over for a couple more days.

After being in Boston for about a fortnight, I wrote to my pen pal. I had a letter in return, inviting me to Charleston, West Virginia, for a holiday. I didn't know what to do. I was having such a wonderful time in Boston and was loath to leave, not knowing what the people in West Virginia were going to be like. After careful thought, I decided it would be a good experience to go – at least I would be able to see New York and Washington on my travels.

I put in for leave to see 'a very old friend'. I spoke to the Captain, told him my story and after some hesitation he granted me 21 days leave. I made arrangements with Jackie to go to Charleston the following weekend. It was my weekend off, so it meant, with my senior chief's permission, I was able to travel down on the Thursday night before my leave was due to start on the Monday at 8am.

I booked my ticket on the Greyhound bus service, the distance being 1000 miles and the fare $22.45. The actual travelling time, not including stops, was 24 hours. This bus service was so efficient that I feel I must say a word about it. You were given a seat number on entering your bus and you kept this number until the end of your journey. You would order refreshments at one terminal and on arrival at the next you sat at a table with your number on it and almost immediately your food, or drink, was put in front of you.

When we arrived at New York, a boy with my seat number on his coat carried my bags to my number cubicle in the station, where I was able to have a good wash and clean up. The boy took my white uniform and shoes away with him and within fifteen minutes was back with my uniform nicely pressed and shoes whitened.

I started my journey on Thursday evening, arriving in New York on Friday morning. I spent a few hours in New York having a look around, then about noon boarded a bus for my second 500 mile journey to Washington and Charleston.

When we arrived at Washington, I rang Jackie to say where I was because I hadn't given her any idea of what time I would be arriving. I told her the bus for Charleston was due to leave and she said "Ask the conductor to put you down at the drug store. I'll be waiting for you." I can't explain the way I felt on the last lap of the journey, not knowing what to expect on arrival, and what sort of people I would be spending a holiday with.

We duly arrived at the drug store at 1am and I alighted to find not a soul about! Then I looked across the road where there was a huge Studebaker car parked. The door opened and out stepped a very beautiful young lady. Any doubts I had before were expelled by what I saw. After a few minutes' chat I got in and we drove to a very imposing house and were greeted by her mother, father and sister. I had a wonderful welcome and my thoughts were, "If this is West Virginian hospitality, I'm glad I left Boston." Mr. and Mrs. Browning were both born in England and were very proud of the fact. They were taken to the United States when babies.

It was late, or rather early morning, when we eventually went to bed and I was hoping for a good night's sleep, not having had much the previous night. At about 9am the following morning, Mrs. Browning woke me and said I had better come downstairs as there were a lot of people waiting to see me. I couldn't understand this at all, but I got up quickly and went downstairs to be faced with reporters and photographers all wanting interviews and my picture. Apparently, Mr. Browning had mentioned my visit to a press friend of his so they knew of my arrival. The last thing my Captain said to me after granting leave was, "Don't talk about the ship and don't discuss the sinking of the *Bismarck*." Facing these chaps, I found this extremely difficult and what I didn't say they surmised, and what I was reported to have said in the papers that evening frightened me to death. I was very fortunate that West Virginian papers weren't circulated in Boston! The whole of that morning was spent being interviewed by various people, one of whom was from the local broadcasting company, asking me to broadcast that evening!

He asked lots of questions about England: were we starving? Just how were the people of England faring, and what did I think would be the ultimate outcome of the war? He then asked me questions about myself – my own feelings during the engagements, what I was doing before the war, which sport I took part in and many other things.

That evening Jackie and I went to Broadcasting House, where we were taken to the interviewing room and eventually the programme was on the air. The announcer started off with these words: "We've got a Bundle from Britain with us in Charleston in the person of Royden Jandrell who lives in a vine hung villa in Wales." Apparently, 'Santos', the name of our house, means 'vine hung' in Spanish. He asked me very similar questions to the interviewers at the house in the morning, and when he asked me which sport I took part in before joining the Royal Navy, I said, "Billiards", and that I was the Welsh champion when I left home. This I may say opened another field for me, and a very profitable one.

The following morning I received a letter from a Mr Evan Evan Evans, who had left Pontypridd many years before and now owned a string of hotels and restaurants in America, but originally he left Pontypridd to start the YMCA in America. Enclosed with the letter was a complimentary card offering me meals and accommodation at any of his hotels during my stay in America. I often met Mr Evan Evan Evans and every time I met him he gave me a $20 bill. I also met many who claimed to be Welsh or who had Welsh connections.

Jackie and I were having a wonderful time. We were entertained in all the best places, and no matter where we went I wasn't allowed to pay for a thing and we were mobbed every time we were recognised. It was during one of these occasions that I had my first encounter with the United States Police. I went into a toy shop to buy a present for my younger brother; Jackie was in the car. When I came out of the shop there were a number of people around the car. They were asking me all manner of questions, when above all the talking I heard a loud whistle. I looked up to see a U.S. policeman coming towards me, brandishing his truncheon and blowing his whistle.

When he reached me, he apologised profusely and said that if he had known it was me, he wouldn't have bothered, but anyone else would have had a ticket. I replied that it was a pity he hadn't served me with a ticket, as I would have liked one for a souvenir. He said he had been a policeman for a good many years and I was the first person to have asked him for a ticket. So, out came his notebook and he put a cross by 'blocking traffic' on a card, with instructions that the fine was to be paid by five o'clock the next day.

After lunch the following day Jackie and I went to the Law Building to pay the fine. I went to the window and handed my summons in to the policeman, who looked at the summons, and then at me, and said, "Aren't you the English sailor visitor?" I told him I was. He immediately called a sergeant, who looked at my summons and shouted to get police officer so-and-so in to ask him "what the hell he was thinking about"! I told him that the responsibility was mine because I had asked for a summons for a souvenir. I was then taken to an inspector, who eventually took me to the Chief of Police. I told him my tale of wanting a souvenir, and he said, "If you wanted a souvenir, why the hell didn't you come to me?" He then asked me how I would like a 'real' souvenir. I said that I would, very much.

The following evening I was being given a civic dinner in honour of my visit to Charleston. My friend Evan Evan Evans, I think, had something to do with the arranging of it. The Chief of Police picked up the telephone and spoke to the mayor and explained all about the summons and asked his permission to give me a real souvenir; in fact, to make me an Honorary Member of the United States Police Force. He must have been agreeable because the following evening I went to the dinner and was presented with the cap badge, breast badge and the relevant cards.

After an unforgettable holiday in Charleston, West Virginia, I was eventually given a wonderful send-off from the bus station by friends and acquaintances I had made during my stay. It was a unique experience and no one would ever dream that so much could happen in such a short time in a foreign country.

I arrived back in Boston after spending 24 wonderful days' holiday with almost three times as much money as I left the ship with, thanks mostly once again to my Welsh friend Evan Evan Evans.

Royden J. Jandrell D.S.M.
HMS *Rodney*

Statement made by Mtr. Gfr. (Ord. Seaman) H. Manthey

About 1700 on Friday 23 May 1941, a smoke cloud was sighted. At this time I was on my action station No. 5 starboard 2-cm gun. Immediately afterwards the enemy cruiser opened fire. The cruiser was astern. *Bismarck* replied with turrets C and D. I do not know how many salvoes were fired. The cruiser thereupon turned off but maintained contact. On the loud speaker system it was announced that the enemy cruiser had made a signal giving *Bismarck*'s position. Half an hour later it was announced that the enemy cruisers were shooting at each other. After that we were relieved. The night was quiet.

At about 0600 on Saturday 24 May, it was announced over the ship's broadcast that smoke clouds had been sighted. Action stations were sounded. Shortly afterwards the smoke clouds could be seen with the naked eye. At this time I belonged to No. 5 port 2-cm gun. On action stations the starboard watch came on and I had to change over to No. 5 starboard 2-cm gun. A few minutes later the first enemy ship opened fire. At this time I did not know which enemy ships were concerned. Shortly afterwards *Bismarck* and a second enemy ship opened fire. The bridge issued an order concerning the distribution of fire. The two forward turrets fired against the *Hood*, whilst the after turrets fired against the *King George V*. The names of the enemy ships were announced after the action. Three salvoes were fired against the *Hood*.

Whilst this firing was going on the anti-aircraft crews were sent under cover because of the splinter effect and the air pressure of our own guns. Out of interest in the battle, however, many comrades remained on deck amidships and in the superstructure. During this firing I myself was under cover (deck house). Already after our second salvo had been fired it was announced "enemy is burning", after the third salvo "enemy is exploding". During this engagement with the *Hood*, the after turrets which were directed from the after control position, had been scoring hits. *King George V* thereupon turned off. *Hood* was sunk about the same time. The general enthusiasm was great. It became still greater when it was announced from the bridge that the enemy were the largest British battleships. At the same time it was announced that *Hood* had been sunk and that *King George V* had turned off. Only now I heard that yet another enemy cruiser was firing on us. The engagement lasted for about another 10 minutes. At the end of the action we learned that *Bismarck* had received three hits. In my opinion these three hits were caused by the last enemy heavy cruiser. One hit in the ship's side (at the bows). The second hit went through the starboard picket boat and detonated in the water. Comrades told me that the third hit had gone into the port oil bunker, compartment XV to XVII. I went there myself and saw that oil was pouring out and was also spilled on the upper deck. The damage itself was under water and could not be seen. This was about 2 hours later.

At this time it could be noticed that the forecastle lay deeper in the water and that the ship had a very slight list to port. I also heard at this time that the electrical engine room No. IV had broken down owing to penetration of water. A little later it was said that the damage had been repaired by divers and damage control parties. A gunner's mate who belonged to my gun said that only the ship's side had been torn open; others maintained that the shell had gone through but had not detonated.

At this time the sea was calm and visibility was good. The ship reduced speed and a collision mat was got out on the forecastle and divers were sent down into the ship to find out the damage. I heard that it had been very difficult to get into the compartments full of water. The divers however succeeded in making a pipe connection to the oil bunkers, so that the oil could be pumped aft. In the meantime they succeeded in stopping the leak. As far as I can remember the outboard work took about 2 hours. The ship then increased speed again. During this time pumping was continued below deck. It was continued the whole day as well as the night. During Saturday morning I noticed that the forecastle was slowly rising again. On Saturday about noon one flying boat appeared. From the type it was first thought to be a Do 18. From talk I heard I know that a recognition signal was demanded and that the aircraft made the correct answer. This was announced through the telephone. When the aircraft approached to within 4,000 metres, the anti-aircraft officer Lt. Cdr. Gellart recognized it as an aircraft of American build. Thereupon the 10.5cm guns opened fire on the aircraft. The aircraft turned off and tried a few more times to approach again but was forced to turn off every time. The aircraft remained then outside the range but maintained contact.

At about 2300, three flights (27 aircraft) of bi-planes appeared to attack. First of all they tried to attack together from port. When they could not succeed in this, they attacked singly from starboard, ahead and astern. All available guns, including the 38-cm guns, participated in the defence.

The attack lasted about an hour and altogether 5 aircraft (according to statements made by my comrades) were shot down. This was confirmed on the order transmission system. I do not know how many aircraft were actually shot down. On my request my anti-aircraft officer Lt. Doelker told me that two flights of torpedo carrying aircraft and one flight of bombers had been involved in the attack. Owing to the continuous zig-zagging (avoiding torpedoes) the anti-aircraft defence was particularly difficult. The aircraft only scored one torpedo hit, starboard amidships, below the aircraft catapult. The torpedo detonated on the ship's side and left merely scratches in the paintwork. Ldg. Seaman Kirchberg who was standing on the starboard 10.5-cm gun was thrown by the air pressure against the hangar and was killed. This was the first fatal casualty onboard. I do not know if other comrades were injured.

Shortly after the end of the engagement with the aircraft *King George V* opened fire on us. *Bismarck* returned the fire with one or two salvoes. As far as I know no hits were scored on either side. As far as I can remember the night of 24/25 was quiet. On the telephone it was announced that the enemy was maintaining contact. On 24 May I was on watch on the gun from 2000–0000.

Prinz Eugen I saw for the last time on the morning of 24 May about 0600, when the action with the *Hood* was in progress. At noon nothing could be seen of her.

About 0300 on Sunday 25 May, it was announced through the telephone that of the 27 enemy aircraft which had attacked us only one had returned to the aircraft carrier. At this time the forecastle was again low in the water. Owing to the violent manoeuvres during the air attack the collision mats had broken and water had again penetrated into the forecastle. Speed was reduced, the sea was fairly rough. The damage control parties worked during the whole of Sunday until the next engagement which was on Monday 26 May in the evening. I do not know if the damage control parties continued to work after this engagement on the evening of 26 May.

On Sunday 25 May, about 1200, the Fleet Commander spoke to the crew. As far as I can remember the Fleet Commander said amongst other things the following: "We were not intended to fight enemy warships but wanted to wage merchant warfare. Through treachery the enemy had managed to find us in the Denmark Straits. We took up the fight. The crew have behaved magnificently. We shall win or die."

After the speech of the Fleet Commander the situation became clear to the crew and the mood became serious.

On Sunday afternoon a second funnel was built. On this occasion the spirits of the crew rose again. It was piped that the non-duty watch was to go into the second funnel to smoke.

Otherwise nothing special occurred on Sunday 25 May.

After the air attack on 24 May, both watches ate and slept on their stations. The stations were not left again until the sinking. Enemy shadowing aircraft (2) maintained contact from Monday morning (1000–1100) onwards. Sometimes they tried to approach closer but were each time forced to turn off by the anti-aircraft defence. As far as I know no recognition signals were exchanged. They were two bi-planes. In the evening between 2100–2200 the anti-aircraft control station reported 16 enemy aircraft at great height over the ship. Repel aircraft stations were sounded. They did not try to attack but flew off again. We did not open fire. About 10 minutes later I saw three enemy aircraft (bi-planes) bearing approximately 200°, approach our ship from the clouds. Immediately afterwards aircraft approached us from all sides. It was fairly cloudy. I do not know the exact number of aircraft. All anti-aircraft weapons opened fire. At this time I felt two heavy shakings in the ship, one shortly after the other.

According to statements of my comrades three depth charges lying on the quarterdeck were thrown overboard by the air pressure of the 38-cm guns which were firing on a torpedo track. I do not know whether the shakings originated from the depth charges. The attack was broken off after about 30 minutes owing to the heavy anti-aircraft fire.

The attacks were dive bombing attacks coming from the clouds down to about 10–20 metres above the water. Generally speaking we had the impression that the attacks were made very pluckily. 7 aircraft were shot down. From the main anti-aircraft control position it was announced: "Rudder jamming hard to starboard. Ship goes in circles". I do not know how many torpedoes hit. In my opinion one torpedo hit went aft into the steering compartment and another hit near compartments VII–VIII. Some men were injured on port gun No. 4. Through the telephone I heard that the divers were trying to couple in the hand rudder. After 20–30 minutes we heard again through the ship's telephone that the hand rudder had been coupled in. Shortly afterwards a second report: Rudder absolutely clear again. Whilst the rudder was out of action it was tried to steer the ship with the screws. As far as I can remember the ship after the hit reduced right down from her cruising speed of 24 knots. She was going in circles. By going astern with the screws the ship was put against the sea. When the hand rudder was coupled in, the ship went first of all 13 knots and later increased to 24 knots.

When cruising at 24 knots enemy destroyers made an attack (from memory at 0000). Action stations were sounded. First of all I did not know whether the attack came from starboard or port, however, I remembered afterwards that it started on the port quarter and a little later shifted to the starboard side. I did not notice that *Bismarck* made an alteration of course. At this time it was announced over the ship's telephone that one destroyer was sinking and two more burning.

I myself did not see anything of this. During action stations which lasted until about 0700 on Tuesday 27 May, the enemy continuously fired starshells. Occasionally it became clear as day. On Monday night various congratulatory telegrams arrived, amongst them one from the Führer awarding the Knight's Cross of the Iron Cross to the Senior Gunnery Officer. The Captain read these telegrams to the crew. Furthermore 81 aircraft were promised for the next day. One U-boat was supposed to be very near to us and all U-boats had been warned. One tanker and two tugs were also on the way to help us. These announcements lifted the morale of the crew again. Many sang. Otherwise nothing on Monday.

About 0200, 27 May 1941, more enemy destroyers had approached to within 3,000 metres. The 38-cm, 15-cm, and 10.5-cm guns were firing. The 3.7-cm and 2-cm guns had orders to wait for special permission to open fire. Of these destroyers one was set on fire; this I observed myself as she was on the starboard beam. Before the attack of the destroyers, i.e., before 0200 an aircraft made a dive-bombing attack from the clouds. Anti-aircraft fire forced the aircraft to turn off. The action with the destroyers lasted until about 0600. No torpedo or gunnery hits were scored. *Bismarck* was making way until this time (0600); I do not know the speed. About 0600 a stand-easy was ordered. I do not know for what reason. She had a slight list to port. Heavy seas. The waves came up to the upper deck. During the night an attempt was made to start the ship's aircraft, but did not succeed. Reason: No compressed air and too much pitching. One aircraft was thrown overboard. It drifted in the water with the floats on top.

During the stand-easy it was piped: All non-duty officers into the charthouse. Immediately afterwards action stations were sounded. Nothing could be seen of the enemy. It was said that smoke clouds had been sighted. Before our own guns fired, enemy shells dropped close to the ship. After about one hour the first hits were scored on our ship. I myself was wearing the telephone. The connection broke off. I took off the telephone. From this time onwards no orders were given by the anti-aircraft control to my gun. As the hits increased the anti-aircraft crews went under cover. We had the impression that we were fired at from all aides. First I was with a group of 20 men in the after gunnery position. After a few hits close by we fled behind the turrets C and D on the upper deck. Before that we threw about 5–6 rafts on the deck below and went with the rafts behind the turrets. Through a hit all rafts except one or two were destroyed. We had now several injured. At this time turret D was still firing.

At this time my comrade Herzog came to me. We saw a carley float between turret C and D. With the help of several others we released it. This carley float we pulled behind turret D. There several comrades left us. Through a hit which went into the water, i.e., the wave, the carley float and we three were thrown overboard. Nobody was actually on the float. We all three swam towards the float. We only succeeded in reaching it after about 15 minutes as hit after hit landed in the water. Nearby another raft was drifting with one injured and 5–6 other comrades. In the carley float we drifted astern. The ship herself we only saw when we were on top of a wave. Once I saw the *Bismarck* was getting a list to port. It appeared that the ship had made a little way to port. Shortly afterwards I could see *Bismarck* no longer, but only a smoke cloud. I did not hear an explosion. Not far from us I saw two cruisers making towards the place where *Bismarck* was. These cruisers were firing. We had nothing to eat or drink in the raft. The raft which in the beginning had been near us had gone out of sight. I do not know what time we were washed overboard. When the sun was directly over us and we had practically given up all hope of being rescued, we sighted a "Kondor" or FW 200. We waved to it but could not ascertain whether we had been seen.

We felt tired. My comrade Herzog had been injured in the foot. In the evening shortly before 1900 a U-boat suddenly surfaced close to us. We were taken onboard and immediately packed into bunks and fed. The U-boat – she was U 74 – searched for two days for survivors. Only corpses and wreckage were sighted.

I do not know about the radar gear. I did not hear anything about it onboard.

I do not know anything about damage to the W/T station. Neither did I see whether the aerials had been shot away.

(Signed) Herbert Manthey.
Mtr. Gfr. (Ord. Seaman)

Note: As with Signals in the Führer Conferences on Naval Affairs 1941, *Prince of Wales* was mistaken for *King George V*.

Report rescued by U 74.
The operation was reported to Hitler on 6 June.

Commander Nigel 'Sharkey' Ward DSC

The first edition of Ward's book *Sea Harrier Over the Falklands* carried the subtitle A Maverick at War. In many ways, this indicated how he was regarded by himself and others during his time in the Royal Navy (1962– 1989). However, others thought this did not detract from the significant achievements of his war career.

Commander Nigel 'Sharkey' Ward DSC, AFC, RN came to prominence when he led 801 Naval Air Squadron during the Falklands War in 1982 from HMS *Invincible*. He flew over 60 combat missions and was credited with three air-to-air kills. His book contains his frank opinion on the decision making of several senior commanders during that war. He controversially questions whether, if followed, their actions may have caused Britain to lose the Falkland Islands.

Ward retired from the Royal Navy in 1989 and moved to Grenada. Here, he was heard by many in 2011, during an interview broadcast on radio with the son of the C-130 Hercules pilot, Ezequiel Martel, shot down by Ward in battle.

Dr G H Bennett, Dr R Bennett and E Bennett

Dr G H Bennett is the author of over a dozen books covering military, diplomatic and maritime history. His works include: *Destination Normandy: Three American Regiments on D-Day; Hitler's Admirals; Survivors: British Merchant Seamen in the Second World War;* and *The RAF's French Foreign Legion: De Gaulle, the British and the Rebirth of French Airpower 1940–1945.* He has worked at Plymouth University since 1992, where he is an Associate Professor of History. Dr Bennett is a Trustee of The Britannia Museum, Britannia Royal Naval College, Dartmouth.

R Bennett joined the Merchant Navy as a 16 year old deck apprentice with the Bank Line in 1945. He later had a career in education before retiring as Reader Emeritus at the University of Derby.

G H and R Bennett have written two books together *Survivors: British Merchant Seamen in the Second World War* (Hambledon, 1999) and *Hitler's Admirals* (United States Naval Institute, 2004).

E Bennett is a film-maker and historical researcher.

Britannia Naval Histories of World War II

Never previously published in this format, documents once stamped 'restricted' have been sourced from Britannia Royal Naval College's Library. These include reports and plans drawn up by serving Royal Navy Officers during and immediately after World War II. BRITANNIA NAVAL HISTORIES OF WORLD WAR II also contain Germany's recorded view of action against the British, with Hitler's comments, as they were typed and filed at the time: the Führer Conferences.

University of Plymouth Press Military History books are available through bookshops and the Internet: www.uppress.co.uk/nav